Jesus Loves Me

by Sandra Godfrey

illustrated by
Becky Radtke

Cover by Becky Radtke

A publication of Silver Burdett Ginn Religion Division

ISBN No. 0-382-30655-4

Standardized Subject Code TA ac

Printing No. 987654321

Shining Star Publications

1204 Buchanan St., Box 399

Carthage, IL 62321-0399

Unless otherwise indicated, the New International Version of the Bible was used in preparing the activities in this book.

Dedicated to

my husband, Kenneth Godfrey;
my children, Kevin and Jonathan;
my mother, Margaret Backstrom;
my sisters (all five);
and countless members of my extended
Christian family—precious expressions of how much Jesus loves me.

TO THE TEACHER/PARENT

I must confess that on busy days I have fallen into a dreadful temptation—serving fast-food lessons to my class. Without stopping to check nutritional content, I have flipped through my materials; pulled out the quickest ideas I could find; and thrown them on the table for my ravenous youngsters to munch, crunch, and consume.

Maybe you know the feeling. My little ones appeared satisfied for the moment with cutting, coloring, and pasting, but I suspected that they might not be getting all the spiritual nourishment they needed. Though fast-food can be fun and tasty, when the meal is over, I always remind myself that a steady diet of it is not good.

Good teachers know the value of stirring up well-balanced lessons: menus that offer milk and meat, like prayer and praise, trust and faith. With proper planning, preparing those meals need not absorb all our time. Sometimes we merely need to remember what we're trying to accomplish. Is our goal to satisfy small appetites for the moment, or is it to nurture Christians for life?

The material in this book was carefully selected to provide you with well-balanced spiritual menus for preschoolers at home, church, and school. Each unit's nutritional value is noted in the lesson title. Scriptural truths are then served in simple stories, finger plays, crafts, songs, and games. Each lesson shows children a way in which Jesus' love is demonstrated to them each day: in God's creation of them and their families, His care and provision, His coming to earth, His gifts of the Bible, prayer, and the church.

You can be encouraged that your lessons are achieving good results when your children respond favorably to these concepts, asking and answering appropriate questions and showing an interest in heavenly things. May your children learn to delight themselves in God, His Son, and His Holy Spirit. I pray this book will help your children "Taste and see that the Lord is good" (Psalm 34:8) and help them grow into His likeness.

TABLE OF CONTENTS

Genesis 1:26-31;
Genesis 2:7; Psalm 139:14

A SPECIAL PICTURE STORY

Copy this story and the story pictures on pages 6-7. Cut the story apart at the dots. Tape each picture to a sheet of construction paper. Tape each part of the story on the back of its matching picture. Hold up the pictures as you read or tell the story.

Squish, squish, squish, squish. Mandy likes to play in mud. She makes mud cakes. She makes mud pies. Have you ever played in the mud? God has too!

••••••••••

One day when the earth was brand new, there were no people. God took some dirt. He shaped it into a man—a special man.

••••••••••

God named the man Adam. At first the man could not walk or talk or sing. Then God did a wonderful thing. He breathed on Adam (breathe out heavily), and Adam came alive.

••••••••••

Adam sat up. He walked. He talked. He laughed. He sang. God loved Adam so much, He made a woman to be Adam's wife. Through them God would make many, many, many people all over the world. And every one would be special.

••••••••••

God made daddies and mommies, big kids and babies. Then one day God had a great idea! He decided to make you. He made your eyes, exactly the color He wanted them to be. He made your nose just the shape He wanted you to have. He made your fingers and your toes.

••••••••••

What else? He made your hair, your ears, your arms, your bones. Wow! Look at you now.

••••••••••

God made you special, like no one else, to be His friend.

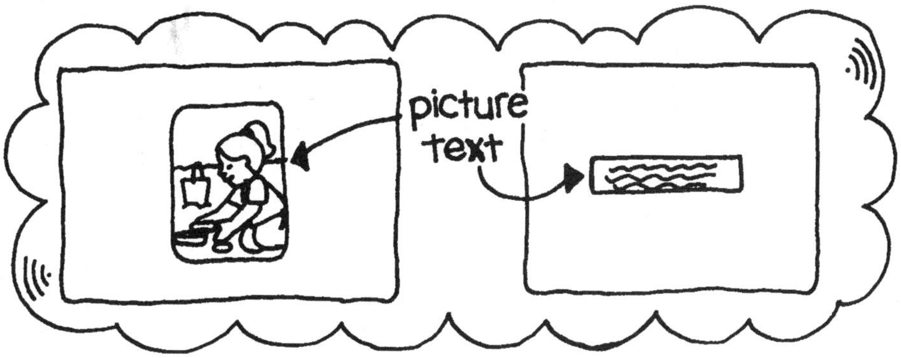

STORY PICTURES

STORY PICTURES

0-382-30655-4

Review Questions:

1. Who was the first person God ever made? *(Adam)*
2. How did God make Adam? *(From the dirt)*
3. Who was Adam like? *(God)*
4. Who made you? *(God)*
5. Why did God make you? *(To be His friend)*

"FOLLOW ME" ACTION GAME

Choose a leader. Help the leader tell the class something special he can do, saying, "God made me special. I can (jump, skip, hop, sleep, share, whistle, growl, etc.)."

All the other children imitate the lead child doing his action. Let the children take turns being the leader.

Bless each child during the game by using word-picture analogies describing their special actions: "God *did* make Nancy special. She can jump as high as a deer." "Jim can snore like a bear." "Ron can hop like a rabbit!"

Reproduce the reward ribbon below and give one to each child for being a good leader.

MAKING ADAM WITH CLAY

Materials: Clay or Play-Doh™
Round cookie cutters (1 small and 1 large)
Paper plate or Styrofoam™ meat tray
Toothpicks or pencils

Directions:
1. Roll the clay out flat like biscuit dough.
2. Cut two large circles for each child—one for the head and one for the body.
3. Cut smaller circles for arms and legs.
4. Help each child assemble a man on a paper plate or meat tray.
5. Put clay through a garlic press to make curly hair.
6. Using toothpicks or pencils, let the children etch Adam's face, fingers, and toes.
7. Talk about how God breathed on Adam and he became a living person.

0-382-30655-4

FINGER PLAY AND ACTION SONG

"My Special Hands"

My hands are very special.	*(Hold hands outstretched.)*
They can help.	*(Wiggle fingers.)*
They can wave.	*(Wave arms high in the air.)*
They can clap.	*(Clap palms together.)*
They can praise.	*(Fold hands in prayer.)*
Thank You, God, for making my hands.	*(Hold hands outstretched.)*

"Face" Song

(Tune: "If You're Happy and You Know It")

1. If you're special and you know it, wiggle your nose.
   If you're special and you know it, wiggle your nose.
   If you're special and you know it, then your face will surely show it.
   If you're special and you know it, wiggle your nose.

2. If you're special and you know it, blink your eyes.
3. Click your tongue.
4. Show your teeth.
5. Pat your cheeks.
6. Thank the Lord.

MEMORY VERSE STAND-UPS

Directions:
1. Reproduce the boy and girl figures below on poster board and cut one out for each child.
2. Have each child color a boy or girl.
3. Stand each figure in a little flattened ball of clay.
4. “Read” the memory verse together several times, clapping hands in the air like cymbals on the word *praise*.
5. Let the children take their memory verse stand-ups home to memorize the verse.

“I will praise you because I am . . . wonderfully made.” Psalm 139:14

0-382-30655-4

"I'M SPECIAL" MIRROR BUTTONS

Hang a mirror in the room or pass around a hand mirror. Let the children look at some special people God made—themselves! Then help them make "I'm Special" Mirror Buttons.

Materials: Poster paper
Foil
Tape
Glitter paint (optional)
"I'm Special" banner pattern (below)
Ribbon

Directions:
1. Cut 4" circles from poster paper, using the pattern below.
2. Cover each circle with foil, taping it in place.
3. Punch two holes in the circle at the top. Cut out the banner and glue it on the circle.
4. Let the children decorate the buttons with glitter paint (especially the stars).
5. Let the decorated buttons dry overnight.
6. Help the children lace ribbon through the buttons to wear as necklaces. Show them how they can look at the buttons and see their faces reflected in the foil.

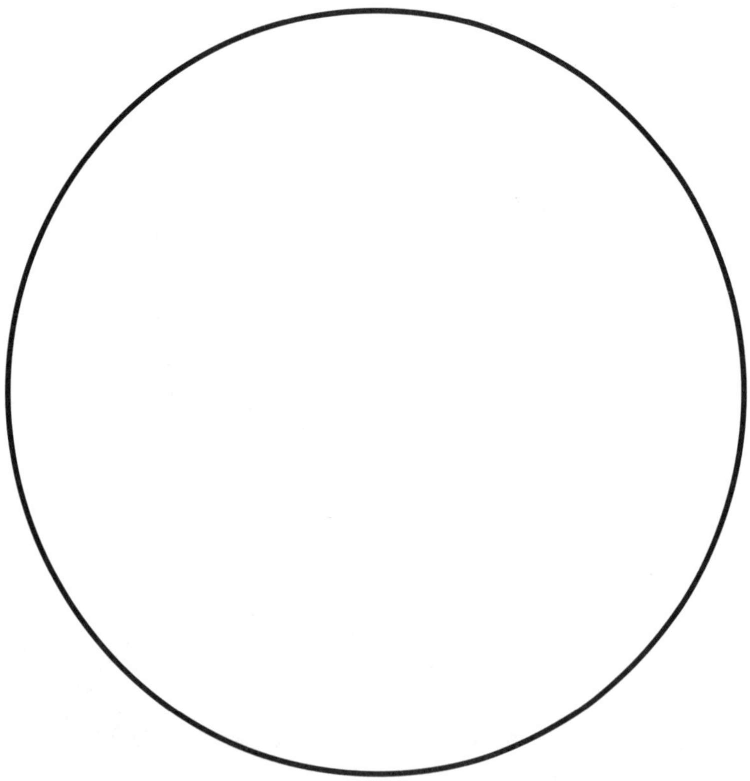

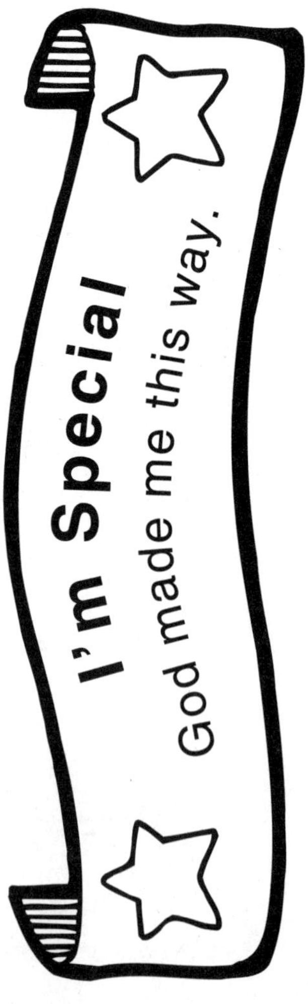

0-382-30655-4

"AROUND THE WORLD" STAMP COLLECTION

Materials:
12" round cardboard circles (such as those in pizza boxes)
Blue and green watercolors
Paintbrushes
"Special People Stamps" (below)
Glue

Directions:
1. Give each child a circle to paint to represent the earth.
2. Cut out the "Special People Stamps" below.
3. Glue the stamps around the earth to represent the many special people God has made.
4. Discuss how all the people around the world are special to God.

0-382-30655-4

FLOWERS IN A BASKET

Materials: Poster paper
Snapshot of each child
Paper cupcake cups
Glue

Directions:
1. Cut flowers from poster paper, using the pattern below.
2. Color the flowers.
3. Take a snapshot of each child.
4. Cut each child's picture to fit the center of a flower.
5. Let the children glue cupcake cups to the center of their flowers; then glue their pictures in the center of the cups.
6. Write the child's name on a flower petal.
7. Help the children display their flowers in a basket.
8. Talk about how we are like flowers in God's garden. People should be reminded of Him when they see us.

NOAH CARES FOR HIS FAMILY

Before telling the following story, help your children make a sound effects cassette tape as described on page 16.

Bam, bam, bam. Wham, wham, wham.

Listen. *(Turn on the cassette of noise 1, hammering.)*

Mr. Noah is building a houseboat!

"A flood is coming," Mr. Noah tells his wife and children. "Water will be everywhere—over houses, over trees. Our home will be inside the big boat."

"Will we be safe?" asks Mrs. Noah.

"Will we be safe?" ask Noah's children, Shem, Ham and Japheth."

"Yes," says Mr. Noah.

But, listen. *(Turn on the cassette of noise 2, laughter.)* Noah's neighbors are laughing at him.

"Build another kind of house," they say, "not a boat!" The whole land looks dry—no clouds in the sky."

But Noah wants to keep his family safe, so he listens when God says, "A flood is coming. Build a boat!"

Listen. *(Turn on the cassette of noise 3, sawing.)*

Noah has been working on the boat for a long, long time.

He built it very wide and very high and very, very, very long. On the top he put a roof. In one side he put a door.

Listen. *(Turn on the cassette of noise 4, animals.)*

"Take animal families into the ark," God told Noah. So, Noah took animals into the boat.

Then into the boat went Noah and his family, and God shut the door. *(Turn on the cassette of noise 5, a door shutting.)*

Listen. *(Turn on the cassette of noise 6, rain.)* What do you hear?

Drip, drop, splitter, splatter. Rain, rain, rain, down it came. The land was flooded with water. But Noah's family stayed safe and dry. Why? Because they listened to God.

0-382-30655-4

MAKING A SOUND EFFECTS TAPE

Tape sound effects for use during the story of Noah. Each sound should last eight to ten seconds. Include the following sounds in this order:

1. Hammering: Let the children use wooden blocks and sticks to make hammering sounds.
2. Laughter: Have the children laugh and laugh and laugh: "heee, heee, ho, ho, ho, heee . . . ."
3. Sawing: Scrape a comb over the edge of a piece of cardboard.
4. Animals: Use wind-up stuffed animals or have the children mimic favorite animal sounds.
5. Door closing: Have a child close the classroom door.
6. Rain: Tap the bottom of cookie pans with fingers.

An Ark to Make and Float

1. Copy the ark below on heavy paper or poster board.
2. Color it with markers.
3. Cover it completely, front and back, with clear adhesive plastic.
4. Use thumbtacks or pins to secure the ark to a floatable bar of soap or a small block of wood.
5. Float the ark in a basin of water.

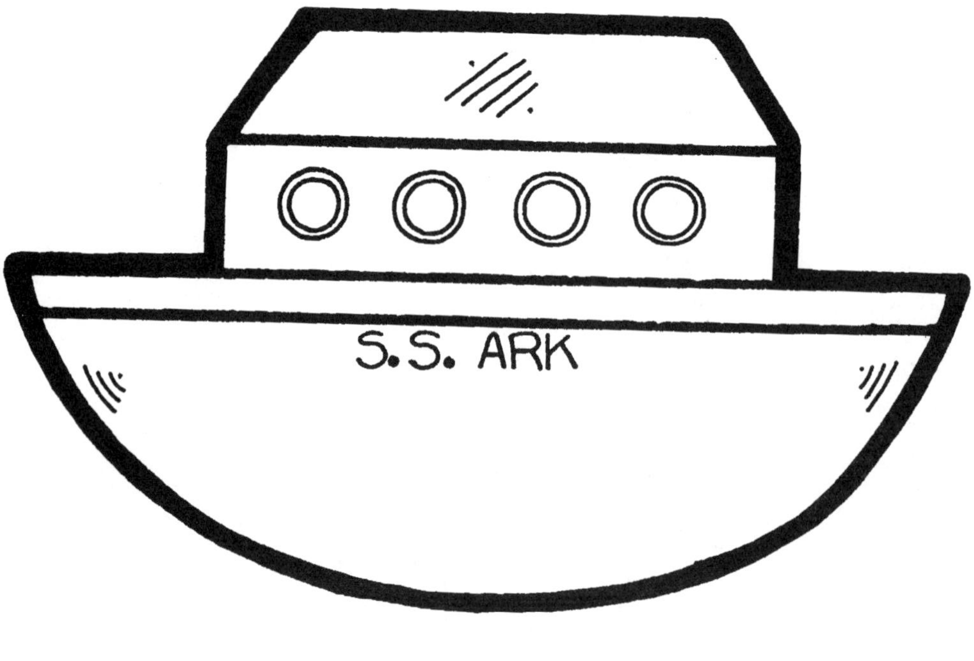

"NOAH'S BOAT" FINGER PLAY

Introduce the finger play by asking the children how they would like living in a boat. Let them discuss other homes God has provided for safety: wooden, brick, mobile, igloo, tent, cave. Pray, thanking God for our families and our homes.

Finger Play Song

(Tune: "Twinkle, Twinkle Little Star")

Noah, Noah build a boat.
Build it strong so it will float.
Take your family inside.
Keep them safely by your side.
Noah, Noah, build a boat.
Build it strong so it will float.

Directions:
1. Wiggle your right index finger to represent Noah working.
2. Cup the fingers of your left hand downward to form the ark.
3. Let the fingers of your right hand be Noah's family. Move them into the boat (left hand).
4. On the last line of the song dip and dive the ark in a waving motion.

A Noah Puppet

Reproduce the Noah puppet pattern below, one for each child. Glue it on sturdy paper. Cut it out, and cut out circles for the fingers. Let the children color their puppets. As you tell how Noah cared for his family (he built the boat and he obeyed God), move the puppet around and let the children imitate your motions. (Your fingers become Noah's legs.)

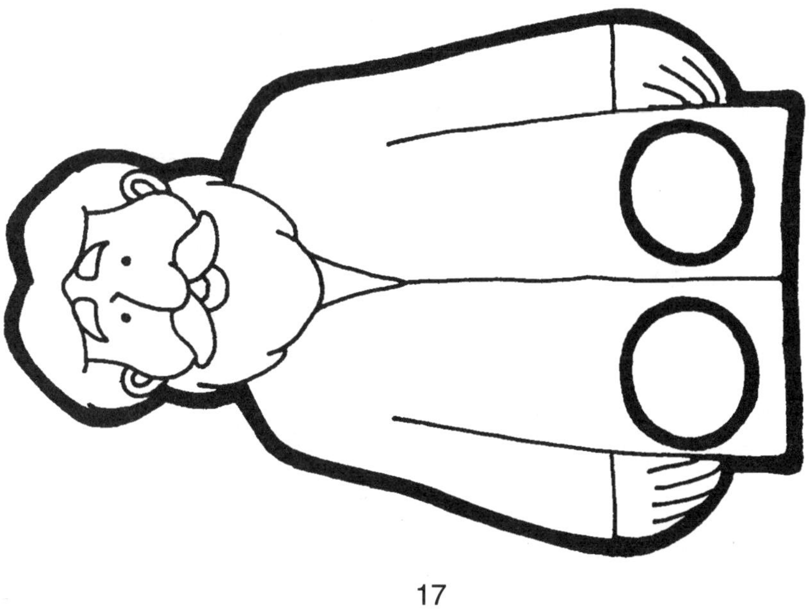

0-382-30655-4

BEANBAG ARK ANIMALS

Let the children make beanbag animals as described below, or provide other beanbags for playing the game on page 19.

Materials: An old mitten, small sock, or zip-up plastic bag for each child
Felt scraps or construction paper
Glue
Large needle
Yarn
Dried beans

Directions:
1. Cut out felt animal features, using the patterns below.
2. Glue the features on the mitten, sock, or plastic bag.
3. Fill the mitten, sock, or bag with dry beans.
4. Tightly seal or stitch the bottom of the beanbag, using a needle and heavy yarn.

0-382-30655-4

BEANBAG QUIZ

Materials: Beanbags
Medium size box

Directions:
1. Help the children form a line several feet behind the box.
2. Ask the first child a question.
3. When he answers correctly, the child may toss his beanbag into the box.
4. Continue until every child gets to answer several questions and toss the bags.

Questions:
1. What did God tell Noah to do? *(Build a boat)*
2. Why did God want Noah to build a boat? *(To keep Noah's family and the animals safe during the flood)*
3. What was the boat like? *(Very long, high, and wide with a door on the side)*
4. What did Noah's neighbors think of the big boat? *(It was silly.)*
5. Why did Noah's neighbors make fun of Noah building the ark? *(There was no rain in sight.)*
6. Who went into the boat? *(Noah, his family, and animals)*
7. How long did it rain? *(Forty days and nights)*
8. How did God take care of Noah's family? *(By shutting them safely in the ark)*
9. Name someone in your family who loves and cares for you.

0-382-30655-4

"FAMILIES" SONG

(Tune: "Hot Cross Buns")

Fam-i-lies,
Fam-i-lies,
Work together,
Play together.
Fam-i-lies.

Fam-i-lies,
Fam-i-lies,
Laugh together,
Pray together,
Fam-i-lies.

"Mother Noah, May I?" Game

God wants families to laugh, play, and have fun together. Let the children tell about some happy times they have shared with their families. Then play the "Mother Noah, May I?" game. Mother Noah needs an apron, a hat, a cloak, or a broom.

Directions:

1. Have the children stand in a horizontal line at one end of the room.
2. The leader, "Mrs. Noah," gives the class an "arkish" command such as, "Take three rabbit hops."
3. The children ask, "Mother Noah, may I?"
4. "Yes, you may," answers Mother Noah.
5. The class members simultaneously take three rabbit hops.
6. The game continues until the class reaches Mother Noah.
7. Additional commands:
   Take two duck waddles.
   Take five worm wiggles.
   Take three cat steps.
   Take one dog jump.
   Take eight bird hops.

MEMORY VERSE MARCH

"Go into the ark, you and your whole family . . . ." Genesis 7:1b

Directions:
1. Using bookcases, benches, or chairs, close in a corner of floor space to represent the ark.
2. Have the children march around the room, saying the Bible verse together.
3. Have the children march into the confined space and sit down.
4. Discuss what work Noah's family did on the ark (cooking, cleaning, feeding and watering the animals).
5. Let them tell work they do with their family (feeding pets, cleaning the lawn, cooking, etc.).
6. Sing "The Family Helper Song" together.

The Family Helper Song

(Tune: "Did You Ever See a Lassie?")

Do you ever help your family,
Your family,
Your family?
Do you ever help your family
Do work at your house?

I wash the dishes. *(Pretend to wash dishes, etc.)*
I sweep the floor.
I play with baby.
I pick up toys.
(Add additional verses the children make up.)

Do you ever help your family,
Your family,
Your family?
Do you ever help your family
Do work at your house?

0-382-30655-4

DOT-TO-DOT ARK

Follow the dots to draw a place where Noah's family found safety. Discuss times when children feel safest at home: during stormy weather, during extreme heat or cold, at night, in danger, in sickness. Tell the children that God gives us families for comfort.

DOT-TO-DOT CHURCH

Tell the children that the church is like the ark. At church people feel loved; they feel safe; they feel close to God and His caring family.

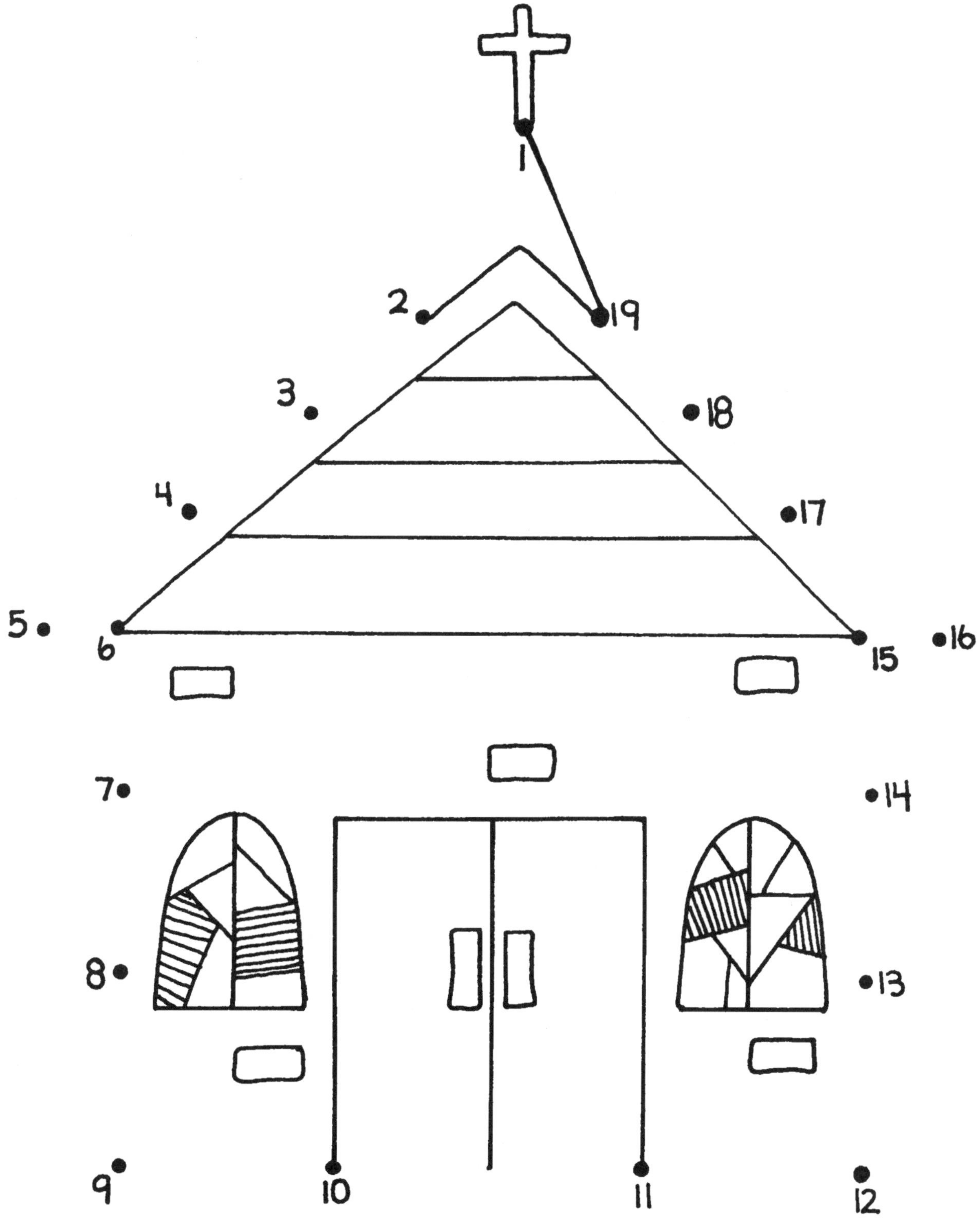

0-382-30655-4

FAMILY PRINTS

Materials: Geometric shapes cut from poster board (Use the patterns below.)
Flat 4" x 4" blocks of wood or small, sturdy cardboard boxes
Glue
Paint
Large sheets of drawing paper

Directions:

1. Show the children how to use geometric shapes to make family members.
2. Glue the shapes on wooden blocks or cardboard boxes.
3. Coat each geometrically shaped person with paint.
4. Stamp the print on paper.
5. Emphasize that we should be good and kind to the people in our family because God sent them to care for us.

0-382-30655-4

THE STORY OF MEPHIBOSHETH

Acting Out the Story

Make stick puppets of Meph (short for Mephibosheth), Ziba, the donkey, and King David, using the patterns on pages 26-27. Drape a cloth over a table, extending it to the floor. Use the puppets to tell the following story from behind the table. Then let the children present the story of Meph in their own words, using the puppets.

"I want to go outside," said Meph. He did not like sitting on the cold floor. He wanted to play in the sunshine.

But Meph could not walk. A woman dropped him when he was a baby and his legs were hurt. Years later he still needed help to get around.

Bam, bam, bam. Someone knocked on the door.

"Come in," shouted Meph. It was Ziba, a servant.

"We must hurry, hurry, hurry," said Ziba. "King David wants to see you at the castle!"

Meph felt scared. "Why does the king want to see me?" he wondered.

Clip-clop. Clip-clop. Clip-clop. Meph rode Ziba's donkey to the castle. There, Meph met the king.

"Meph," the king said in a kind, deep voice, "God wants me to help you. How would you like to move to the city? You could eat food at my table. You could wear good clothes. Many people would help you."

"Oh, thank you, thank you, thank you, Mr. King," said Meph. "I think I will."

Happily, Meph moved to the city. He ate at the king's table. He wore nice clothes. Best of all, many people helped him.

Did God take good care of Meph? Yes, he did!

And God takes good care of you too!

0-382-30655-4

STORY PICTURES

Mephibosheth

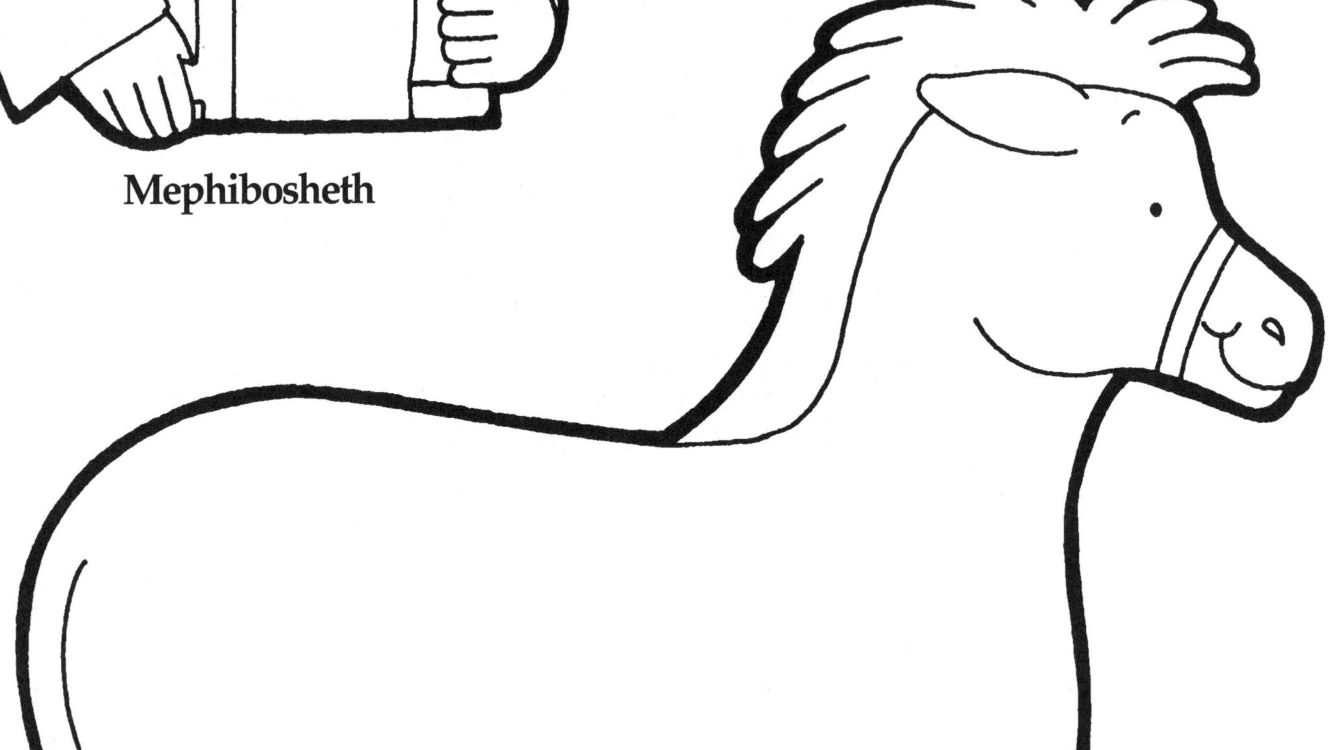

STORY PICTURES

King David

Ziba

0-382-30655-4

"GOING TO THE CASTLE" MAZE

Enlarge the following maze to bulletin board size. Display it within easy reach of the children. Cut out the picture of Mephibosheth on the donkey (page 29) and laminate it. Let the children take turns clip-clopping Mephibosheth on his journey to King David's castle.

Alternate activity: Reproduce the maze for each member of the class. Let the children trace Meph's journey with their fingers.

MEMORY VERSE CASTLES

Copy and cut out this memory verse castle and the peekaboo picture page (page 31) for each child. Cut the castle doors and windows on the dotted lines. Tape the two pages together so the peekaboo people are directly behind the doors and windows of the castle. Let children try to find Mephibosheth. Read the memory verse aloud and help children recite it several times.

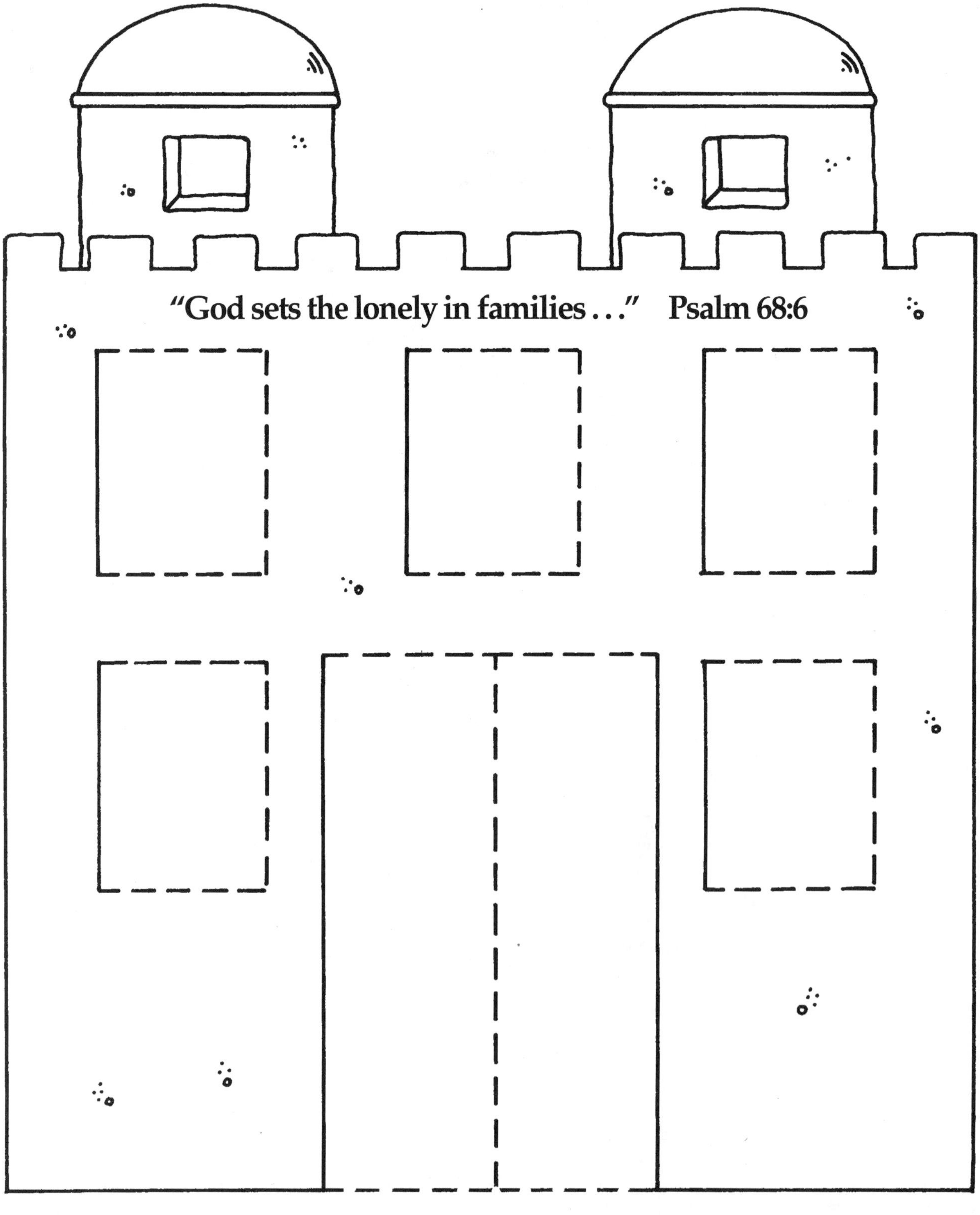

PEEKABOO FIGURES

0-382-30655-4

STAINED-GLASS PRAYER PICTURE

Materials: Art tissue paper
Window pattern, page 33
Prayer inset, below
Poster paper
Scissors
Water
Glue

Directions:

1. Trace and cut the stained-glass window pattern, page 33, from poster paper for each child.
2. Copy and cut out the prayer inset below for each child.
3. Cut several colors of tissue paper in tiny pieces like confetti and put them in a box.
4. Dilute the glue with water in a bowl (half and half).
5. Dip the tissue, piece by piece, in the glue mixture. Layer it on the poster paper window.
6. Let the window dry.
7. Glue the prayer inset in the middle of the window.
8. Fold in the sides of the window on the dotted lines to make it stand up.
9. Pray the prayer, letting your children echo it line by line.

Thank You, Jesus,
That You care for me.
Thank You for
my food,
my clothes,
my friends,
my church,
and my family.
In Jesus' name,
Amen

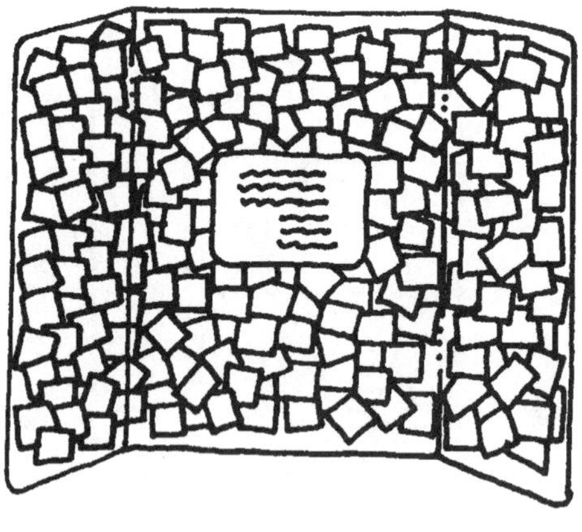

STAINED-GLASS WINDOW PATTERN

GOD'S CARE SONG

Teach the children the following song. Practice it several times. Make a tape of them singing it twice; then play it back and listen to it together.

(Tune: "The Farmer in the Dell")

God takes good care of birds. *(Wave arms like wings.)*
God takes good care of flowers. *(Cup hands around face.)*
God takes good care of families. *(Hug a friend.)*
God takes good care of me. *(Hug self.)*

Me-phib-o-sheth Action Game

Directions:

1. Tell the class that Meph is a short way of saying Mephibosheth.
2. Practice saying his name together.
3. Explain the rules of the game.
   a. When the leader says "Me-phib-o-sheth," the children squat down.
   b. When the leader says "King David," the children hop up.
   c. When the leader says "donkey," the children say "hee-haw."
4. When a child can pronounce Me-phib-o-sheth, she becomes the leader.

Review Questions

1. What was Mephibosheth's problem? *(He could not walk.)*
2. Where did Mephibosheth go? *(To the king's castle)*
3. What did the king want? *(To help him)*
4. What did the king say? *(He could eat at the king's table.)*
5. How did God take care of Mephibosheth? *(By giving him food, clothes, friends)*
6. How does God take care of you? *(He provides for all my needs.)*

0-382-30655-4

"EVERYTHING WE NEED" POSTER

Remind your children that God gives us everything we need to live. Make a class poster, showing some essential needs. Divide it into four sections labeled food, clothes, home, love. Copy the pictures below. Let the children cut them out, color them, and glue them on the poster in the correct places.

0-382-30655-4

"AT THE KING'S TABLE" SNACK

"You prepare a table before me . . . ." Psalm 23:5

Spread a tablecloth on a table. Light a candle and set it in the middle. Serve fruit, cheese, and crackers. Make a crown for each child to wear as you pretend to eat at King David's table.

King David Crowns

Materials: Poster paper
Scissors
Glue
Glitter paint

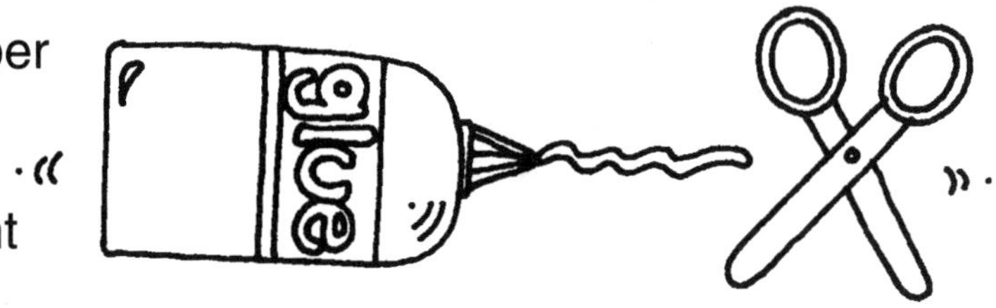

Directions:

1. Cut headbands (approx. 2" x 24") from heavy paper.
2. Cut three triangles per crown.
3. Glue the triangles, slightly overlapping, in the center of the headband.
4. Decorate the crowns with glitter paint.
5. Tape each crown to fit a child's head.

0-382-30655-4

MAKING THE WORLD STORY

Illustrate this story, using a globe draped in a black cloth. Copy and enlarge the pictures on pages 38 and 39. As you tell the story, let the children put together a small bulletin board or poster by assembling pictures of things God created.

Making the World

Once the world was dark and empty and lonely. *(Show the black draped globe.)* It had no plants, no animals, no people.

Then God looked at that dark, lonely world and thought, "I will change the world into a beautiful place."

So God started making new things.

First God said, "Let there be light." And poof—there was light.

Do you know what else God made? *(Begin to build the bulletin board.)* He made:

1. Daytime and nighttime
2. Skies with fluffy clouds floating by
3. Water splashing in oceans, rivers, lakes, and streams
4. A bright, yellow sun
5. A soft, round moon
6. Green plants—trees, bushes, flowers and grass
7. Fish a-jumping
8. Birds a-flying
9. Animals that walk and run and hop
10. Moms and dads
11. Boys and girls

(Take the drape off the globe and spin it.)

Yes, God made this colorful world with things for us to see, to feel, to hear, to smell, to taste. And it was good. Everything God made was very good.

Aren't you glad God make the world? What a great place to live!

0-382-30655-4

BULLETIN BOARD PATTERNS

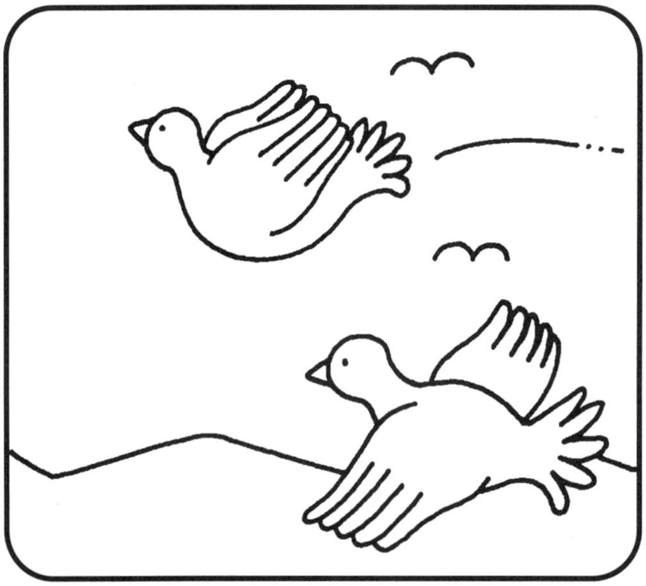

BULLETIN BOARD PATTERNS

"WHAT AM I?" RIDDLES

1. God made me.
   I shine.
   I am big, round, and yellow.
   What am I? *(the sun)*

2. God made me.
   I am blue and white.
   I live way up high.
   What am I? *(sky, clouds)*

3. God made me.
   I am filled with swirling water.
   What am I?
   (ocean, lake, river, stream)

4. God made me.
   I am green with leaves.
   What am I?
   (trees, bushes, grass, flowers)

5. God made me.
   I light up the night sky.
   What am I? *(moon, stars)*

6. God made me.
   I swim in water.
   What am I? *(fish)*

7. God made me.
   I fly in the sky.
   What am I? *(bird)*

8. God made me.
   I have four feet.
   I can run and jump.
   What am I?
   (cat, dog, tiger, etc.)

SPONGE-PAINTED TREE HOUSES

Tell the children that God made trees as homes for many animals: birds, monkeys, frogs, squirrels. Ask how they would like to live in a tree. Talk about tree houses they have visited or seen. Make a class tree for small animals.

Materials: Tempera paint (green and brown)
Sponges
Large sheet of butcher paper

Directions:
1. On a large sheet of paper sketch a huge tree. (See diagram below.)
2. Cut sponges into leaf and bark shapes.
3. Let the children dip their leaf-shaped sponges in green paint and blot them on the top of the tree (or use many colors for autumn).
4. They may dip the bark-shaped sponges (uneven rectangles) in the brown paint to color the tree trunk.
5. Where are the animals? Hiding in the leaves. (You may want to provide animals and birds cut from magazines for children to glue on the tree.)

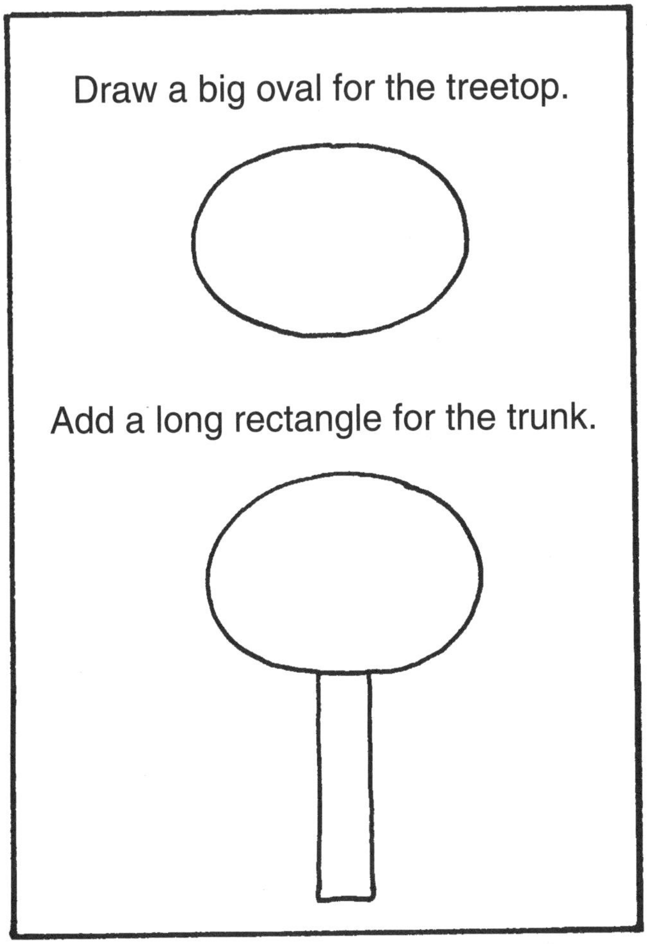

0-382-30655-4

CREATING WILD THINGS

Explain the differences between tame and wild animals. Some of the animals God made do not live near people, but in woods and forests. Name some wild animals together (raccoons, squirrels, rabbits, tigers, lions, deer, antelope, zebras, elephants, etc.). Challenge the children to think up wild animals they would like to create. Give them clay and let them create and name wild animals.

A Thank-You Chain

Make a thank-you creation chain as a class.

Materials: Strips of 1" x 5" colored paper
Glue or tape

Directions:

1. Lay strips of colored paper on the table.
2. Let each child tell something about the world God made for which she is thankful.
3. Each may choose a colored strip.
4. The strips should be taped together into a thank-you chain.
5. When the chain is finished, lead the children in a prayer of thanksgiving for the wonderful world God made.
6. Hang the chain in your classroom.

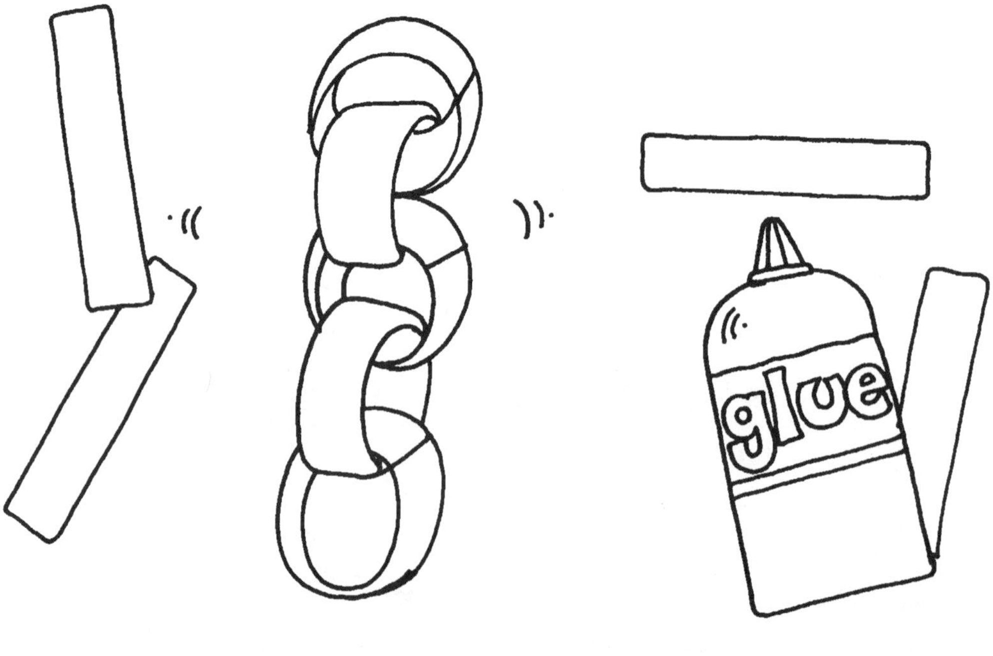

TAME ANIMALS

Remind your children that God made all the animals in the world. Let them tell about their animal pets. Lead the children in giving thanks for animals. Then make tame animals.

Materials: A puppy below cut from folded paper, one for each child
Scissors
Paper plate
Glue
Black crayon

Directions:

1. Cut a puppy from folded paper. Lay the top of the head on the fold. Do not cut across the fold. (When it's finished, the puppy will stand up like a tent.) Use the black crayon to draw an eye, ear, nose, and mouth.
2. Fold the tabs under the puppy's feet.
3. Glue the puppy standing up on a paper plate.

GOD'S GREEN PLANTS

1. Remind the children how wise God was to make so many kinds of plants.
2. Bring samples of edible plants to class: turnip greens, lettuce, cabbage, celery, radishes, beans, peas, fruit. Discuss how we get food from the plants God made.
3. Invite a farmer to visit and tell what he does when farming for food.
4. Serve fresh fruit—strawberries, apples, bananas, etc.—with the following dip.

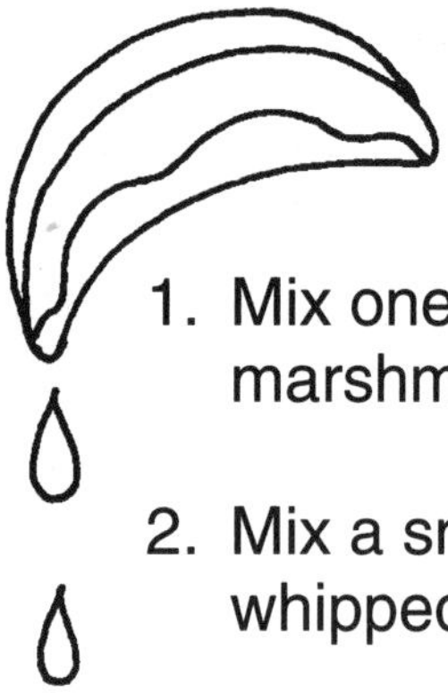

Fruit Dip Recipes

1. Mix one 4-ounce package of cream cheese with a jar of marshmallow cream or melted marshmallows.

2. Mix a small container of fruit-flavored yogurt with a small carton of whipped cream.

Leaf Hike

Take a hike outside. Marvel over the things God has made: the blue sky; the brilliant sunshine; the quick, colorful birds; the tall green plants. Give every child a small paper sack in which to collect a variety of leaves. Then go back inside and make leaf prints.

Leaf Prints

Materials: Leaves
Large sheets of drawing paper folded in half
Crayons

Directions:
1. Place the leaves inside folded paper.
2. Have the children color roughly on the front of the paper to see their leaf prints appear.
3. Point out the variety in the leaves God made.

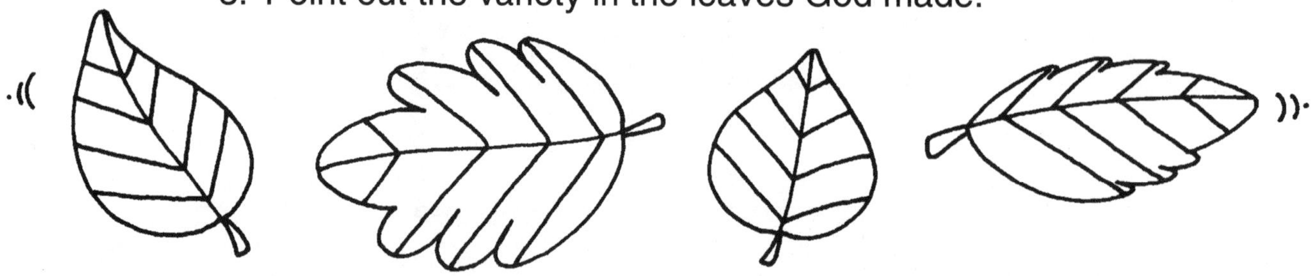

0-382-30655-4

WATER PLAY

Ask, "What is so wonderful about water?" (You can swim in it, drink it, freeze it, bathe in it, cook with it, mix things with it, float things in it. You can see through it. You cannot taste clean water or smell it, but you must have it to live!) Tell the children that God was very wise to make a special thing like water.

Materials: Large water basin half filled with water
Objects that float and others that won't
(nail, pencil, paper clip, assorted toys)

Directions:
1. Let the children take turns dropping objects into the water to see what floats.
2. Remind them that only God could have thought of water!

Thanking God for a Rainbow World

Play "I Spy." Let a child give hints about something he sees, giving only the color of it. The class gets three guesses to find out what it is. Talk about the many colors God made. Then make the color worlds described below.

Color Worlds

Materials: Coffee filters
Food coloring and water mixed in small bowls or cups

Directions:
1. Fold the coffee filters into eighths.
2. Dip each triangular edge into a different food color. Then dip the point into a color.
3. Unfold the coffee filters. The colors will "bleed" toward the center.
4. Allow them to dry; then display them.

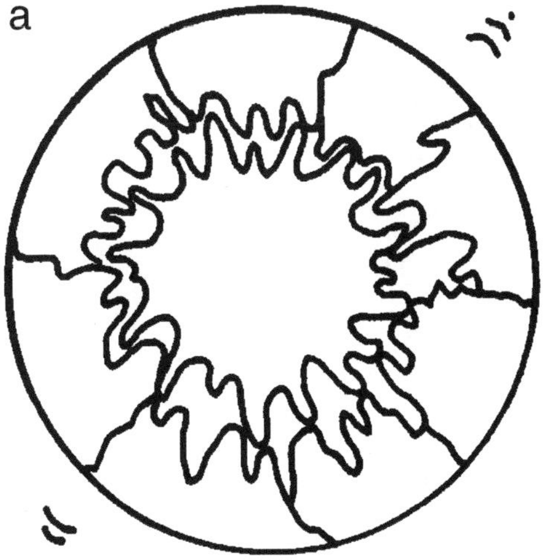

"IT WAS GOOD" SONG

(Tune: "Deep and Wide")

Chorus:

It was good.
It was good.
Everything God made was good.
It was good.
It was good.
Everything God made was good.

Verses with motions:

1. Ducks were good. *(waddle)*
   Ducks were good.
   All the ducks God
   made were good.
   Ducks were good.
   Ducks were good.
   All the ducks God
   made were good.
2. Cats were good.
   (Stroke arm like cat.)
3. Trees were good.
   (Sway arms like limbs.)
4. Water was good.
   (Pretend to drink.)
5. Encourage the children to suggest alternate verses and motions.

Final verse:

God is good.
God is good.
Our God is very, very good.
God is good.
God is good.
Our God is very, very good.

Memory Verse

"And God saw all that He had made, and it was very good." Genesis 1:31

Finger Play

God made the world to touch, *(Draw a big circle with finger.)*
To taste, *(Lick lips.)*
To smell, *(Sniff with nose.)*
To hear, *(Cup ear with hand and say shhhhh.)*
To see. *(Put fingers around eyes like glasses.)*
Thank You, God, for making me. *(Point to self.)*

SURROUND SOUND

Bring a rocking chair to class. Sit in the chair to tell the story. Have a picture of the nativity scene or a creche. Before the story, tape the figures from page 48 on separate pieces of construction paper. Hold up the figures and let the children rehearse making sounds for the animals. As you tell the story the children will repeat the animal sounds when you hold up the figures.

Carie's Favorite Story

"My favorite story in the whole world is the story of Baby Jesus," said Carie. "Please," she asked her grandmother, "tell it one more time."

Nana's chair softly creaked as Carie wiggled into her lap. Back and forth Nana rocked.

"Moooo," said the cows in the little stable.

"Coooo," said the doves roosting in the loft.

"Hee-haw," said the donkey, nibbling golden hay.

"Baaaa," said the sleepy white lamb in the corner.

"Ahhhh," said Mary as she watched her new little baby. Quietly He slept in a manger filled with hay.

"Isn't He precious?" asked Joseph.

"Yes," said Mary.

Gently Mary rubbed the baby's soft, brown hair.

"Dear little Jesus," she said, "God's Son—our Savior. I'm so happy You came tonight."

"Moooo," said the cows in the darkened stable.

"Coooo," said the doves roosting in the loft.

"Hee-haw," said the donkey, nibbling golden hay.

"Baaaa," said the sleepy white lamb in the corner.

"Ahhhh," said Mary.

"Ahhhh," said Joseph.

"Ooooo," said the baby who had come to bring God's love to everyone.

"One more time, Nana," said Carie. "Please? Tell that story one more time."

Nana rocked and smiled. Once more she told Carie how God's Son was born in a stable.

0-382-30655-4

STABLE ANIMAL PICTURES

0-382-30655-4

MEMORY VERSE BANNER

"A Savior has been born to you; He is Christ the Lord." Luke 2:11

Materials: A 12" x 12" square of white felt for each child
Hearts cut from red felt (patterns below)
Silhouette of Jesus in the manger cut from black felt (pattern below)
Copy of the memory verse strip above
Yarn

Directions:
1. Arrange the hearts, Baby Jesus figure, and verse on the white felt.
2. Glue the pieces in place.
3. Punch holes in the top two corners of the felt and knot yarn through both to make hangers.
4. Teach the children the memory verse. Repeat it several times.

0-382-30655-4

"WHERE IS BABY JESUS?" GAME

Directions:
1. Make stars, one for each student, using the pattern below.
2. Choose a child to be "it."
3. "It" turns his back to the class.
4. Give a star secretly to someone in the class.
5. That child conceals the star.
6. "It" gets three chances to guess who has the star. When he guesses correctly, he receives the star and a new "it" is selected.
7. Play until each child has received a star.
8. Talk with the children about the star that helped the wise men find Baby Jesus.

Baby Jesus in a Manger

Materials:
- A 2" Styrofoam™ ball for each child
- Brown markers
- Chenille stems
- Small white felt square (one for each child)
- 5" baskets or small boxes
- Straw, hay, or curled paper strips

Directions:
1. Draw sleepy facial features on the ball for the baby's head.
2. Bend chenille stems to make a body.
3. Wrap the baby in a white "felt" blanket.
4. Fill the basket with hay.
5. Put the baby in the manger basket.

CLAY MANGER SCENE

Let children form figures from clay to make a class nativity scene. Provide a box strewn with straw or hay and figurines for Mary, Joseph and, Baby Jesus. Let the children add cows, doves, donkeys, and lambs.

Review Questions

1. Where was Jesus born? *(In a stable)*
2. Who was Jesus' mother? *(Mary)*
3. Who was Jesus' father? *(God)*
4. Why did Jesus come to earth? *(To bring God's love to everyone)*

"God Is Love" Song

(Tune: "Are You Sleeping?")

String jingle bells on yarn so the children can play them while they sing.

God so loved the,
God so loved the,
world, world, world,
world, world, world,
He-ee sent His only Son.
He-ee sent His only Son.
God is love.
God is love.

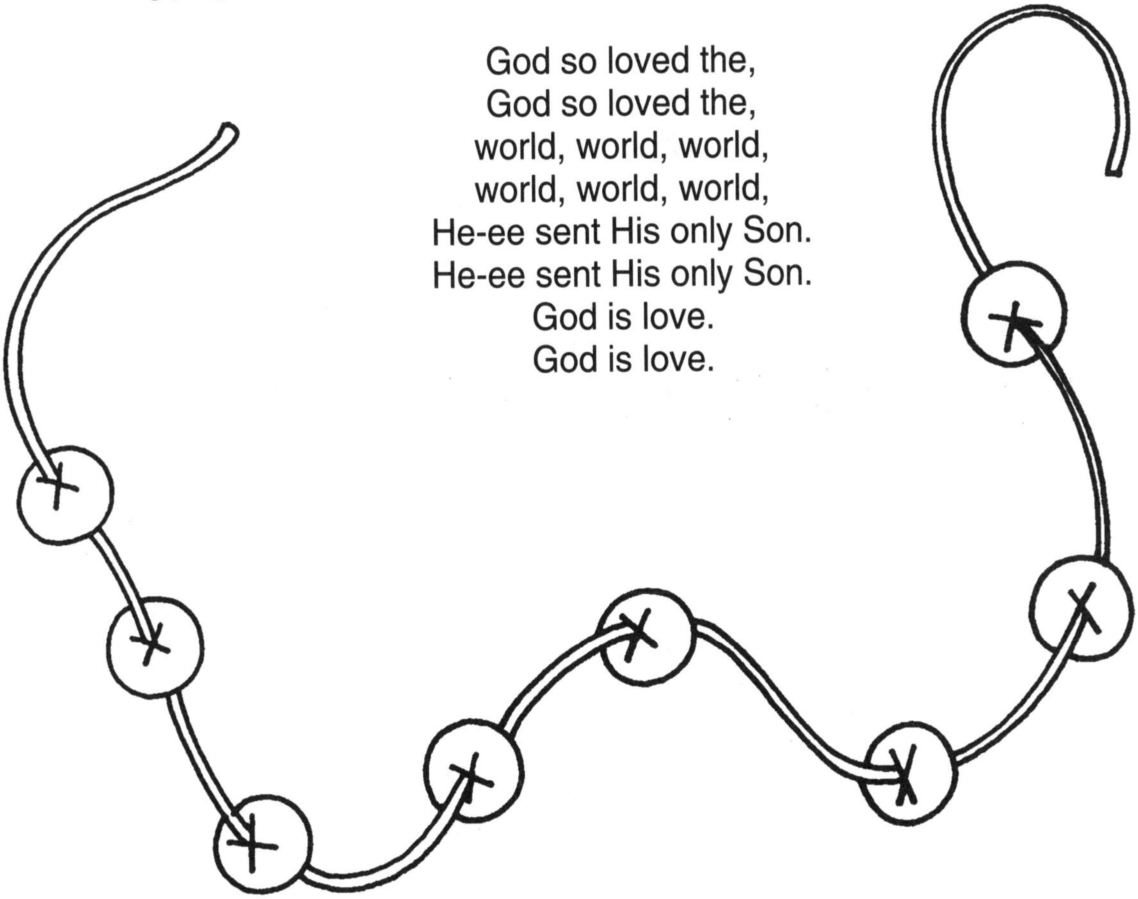

0-382-30655-4

"JESUS LOVES ME" COLORING BOOK

Copy the pictures on this page and page 53 for a coloring book for each child. Cut out the pages and staple them together. Look at the pictures together, discussing how Jesus came to earth as a little child and grew up, showing God's love to all people everywhere. Let the children color the pictures.

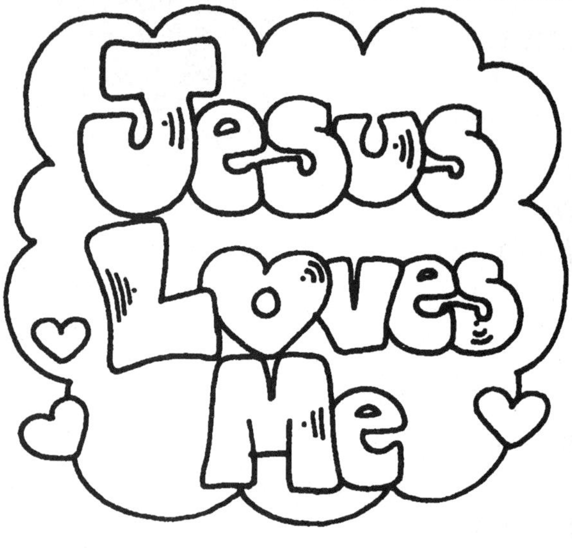

____

Name

Baby Jesus was born in a stable in Bethlehem.

1

He was God's very own Son.

2

Mary and Joseph loved Jesus very much.

3

0-382-30655-4

They took good care of Him as He grew up.

4

Jesus told people about God's love.

5

Jesus died on a cross so we can go to heaven.

6

Jesus loves everyone! And Jesus loves you!

7

SONG

(Tune: "Head and Shoulder, Knees, and Toes")

1. Why did Jesus come to earth?
   Come to earth?
   Come to earth?
   Why did Jesus come to earth?
   To say, "God loves you."

2. Why did Jesus heal the sick?
   Heal the sick?
   Heal the sick?
   Why did Jesus heal the sick?
   To say, "God loves you."

3. Why did Jesus calm the storm?
   Calm the storm?
   Calm the storm?
   Why did Jesus calm the storm?
   To say, "God loves you."

4. Why did Jesus feed the hungry?
   Feed the hungry?
   Feed the hungry?
   Why did Jesus feed the hungry?
   To say, "God loves you."

5. Why did Jesus hug the children?
   Hug the children?
   Hug the children?
   Why did Jesus hug the children?
   To say, "God loves you."

Finger Play

Let us walk to the Bethlehem stable.	*(Walk fingers on palm of hand.)*
See Baby Jesus sleeping in the manger?	*(Cup hand above eyes.)*
Tell Jesus, "Thank You for coming to earth."	*(Fold hands in prayer.)*
Feel His love from that holy birth.	*(Cross hands over heart.)*

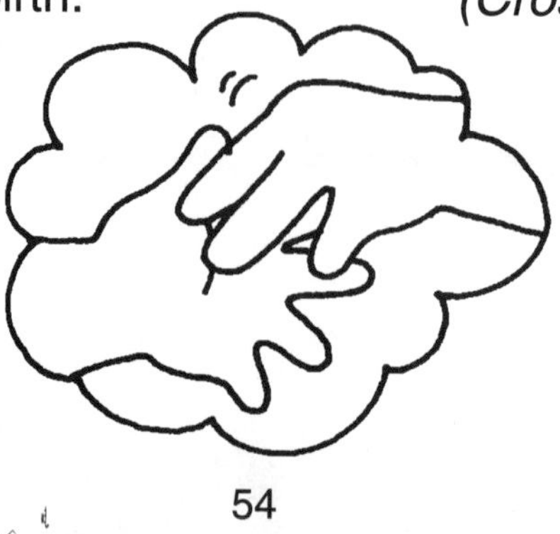

0-382-30655-4

MOSES ON THE MOUNTAIN

Illustrate this story by making flannel board figures of Moses, the mountain, lightning, smoke, trumpets, and tablets of stone.

Tell the Ten Commandments in the story as a finger play. Have the children hold up a finger and echo each of the Ten Commandments as you say it.

Early one morning Moses and God's people gathered at Mount Sinai. It was a very special day. Moses was going up the mountain. He was going to talk with God.

Suddenly lightning cracked. Thunder boomed. A trumpet blasted. The mountain smoked, and all God's people trembled.

"Wait here," Moses told the people. "I will go and talk with God."

Up, up, up Moses went.

"I am the Lord your God." God said to Moses:

1. Worship Me.
2. Do not make other gods to worship.
3. Use My name only in good ways.
4. On God's day, rest and think about Me.
5. Love your moms and dads.
6. Love your husbands and wives.
7. Don't kill.
8. Don't steal.
9. Don't tell lies.
10. Don't wish for what other people have.

With His finger, God wrote His words on tablets of stone. Then Moses carried God's words down the mountain. Now the people had God's rules written down so they could do what was right.

The story of Moses is in the Bible. God gave us the Bible so we can remember to live for Him too.

0-382-30655-4

FLANNEL GRAPH PICTURES

FLANNEL GRAPH PICTURES

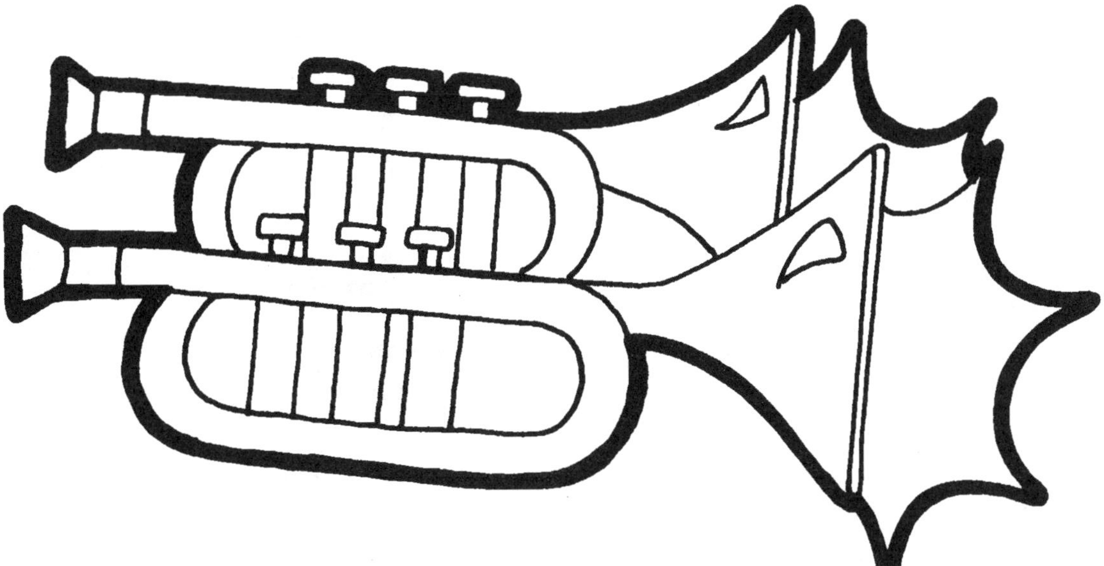

MEMORY VERSE HEARTS

"I have hidden your word in my heart." Psalm 119:11a

Materials: Large heart pattern traced on red construction paper for each child
Tiny Bible pattern traced on black paper for each child
Red ribbon
Copy of Bible verse below

Directions:
1. Cut and fold the small Bibles.
2. Glue a ribbon inside each small Bible for a bookmark.
3. Glue the Bible on the top half of the heart.
4. Cut out the Bible verse and glue it below the Bible. Say the Bible verse together several times.

"I have hidden your word in my heart." Psalm 119:11a

0-382-30655-4

"YES AND NO" ICE-CREAM CONES

Materials: Smiley face and frowny face cones, (below) copied and cut from sturdy paper

Directions:
1. Let each child color a smiley and a frowny face ice-cream cone.
2. Read the true and false statements below.
3. Have the children raise their smiley cones for true statements and frowny cones for the false ones.

True/False Statements

1. The sun is blue.
2. Grass grows in the sky.
3. A dog can fly.
4. A cat can sing.
5. A Mom can cook.
6. A boy can ride a bike.
7. The Bible is God's Word.
8. The Bible will last forever.
9. The Bible makes us strong and brave.
10. The Bible is more special than gold.

"THE BIBLE" SONG

(Tune: "Here We Go 'Round the Mulberry Bush")

Directions: Teach children the song. Then march around the room, following the leader, swaying in time with the music until the last line of each verse. On the last line, children squat to touch the floor, then hop up and lift their hands high in the air.

The Bible is the Word of God,
The Word of God,
The Word of God.
The Bible is the Word of God.
I read it every day.

The Bible tells me of God's Son,
Of God's Son,
Of God's Son.
The Bible tells me of God's Son.
I read it every day.

The Bible fills my heart with joy,
My heart with joy,
My heart with joy.
The Bible fills my heart with joy.
I read it every day.

The Bible is my favorite book,
My favorite book,
My favorite book.
The Bible is my favorite book.
I read it every day.

Studying the Bible

Provide picture Bibles for your children to enjoy. Let them find favorite Bible story pictures. Encourage them to share details of their favorite stories: Adam and Eve, Noah, Daniel, David and Goliath. Tell them to notice the many pictures of Jesus, God's Son. Ask children to explain why there are so many pictures of Jesus in the Bible. (He is the most special person in the Bible!)

0-382-30655-4

"PASS THE TRUMPETS" CRAFT AND GAME

Materials: Set of "Good Word" cards from below
Cardboard cylinders, about 5" long for each child
Watercolor paints and paintbrushes (optional)
Markers

Directions:
1. Reproduce and cut out one set of the Good Word cards.
2. Give children cardboard cylinders (gentle trumpets).
3. Let them decorate their trumpets with paint or markers.
4. Explain the game:
   a. A child chooses a Good Word card and gives it to the teacher.
   b. The teacher whispers the card's message in the child's ear.
   c. The child whispers the Good Word to his neighbor through his gentle trumpet.
   d. When everyone has passed the message along, the class shouts the good news, using their trumpets.

Jesus loves me.

I love Jesus.

God's Word is true.

The Bible makes me strong.

God's Word is forever.

0-382-30655-4

SALT CHALK SCULPTURE

Discuss how Moses climbed Mount Sinai to talk with God. Jesus also talked with God on mountains. Tell the children that mountains are high, high hills—beautiful and quiet. God gave us parts of the Bible from the tops of high mountains (such as the Sermon on the Mount).

Mountains in a Jar

Materials:
- Colored chalk
- 2 or more boxes of salt
- Paper towels
- Small jar for each child
- Package of paper cups

Directions:
1. Give each child a paper towel.
2. Pour about one-half cup of salt on each towel.
3. Show the children how to rub chalk through the salt to color it.
4. Save each child's colored salt in an individual paper cup.
5. Repeat this process several times, making different colors until enough salt has been colored to fill each child's jar.
6. Gently pour the colors one at a time into the jar.
7. If necessary, slide a toothpick down the side of the jar to make mountainous shapes.
8. Be sure to tell the children not to shake their jars!

0-382-30655-4

LESSON QUESTIONS ABOUT THE BIBLE

Use a rope to make a winner's circle in the middle of the floor. Let the children take turns answering questions about the Bible. When one answers correctly, let her stand in the winner's circle until the next child answers a question correctly.

1. What is the Bible? *(A book about God and His people)*
2. Tell something that is in the Bible. *(God's words, stories)*
3. Who is the most special person in the Bible? *(Jesus, God's Son)*
4. How should we treat the Bible? *(With care)*
5. Who gave us the Bible? *(God)*
6. Why do we read the Bible? *(To learn about God and Jesus)*

"The Bible" Finger Play

I hold the Bible in my hands. *(Hold out hands together.)*
I read about God's loving plan. *(Move finger as if reading type.)*
I listen as He speaks to me. *(Cup hands behind ears.)*
I'm happy, happy as can be. *(Clap hands.)*

0-382-30655-4

MAKING ONE OF THE TEN COMMANDMENTS

Materials: Tablet of Stone cut from poster paper for each child, from the pattern on page 65
Copy of the picture below for each child

Directions:
1. Cut out, color, and glue the picture below on the tablet of stone from page 65.
2. Tell children that this is the first and the most important of all God's commandments. God wants us to love and adore Him more than anyone or anything else.

COMMANDMENT PATTERN

A LIVING MURAL

How would you have felt if you had been there when Moses brought God's written commandments down from the mountain? Ask children to think about that question as they work on this mural.

Materials: Mural paper
Colored markers
Instant camera (optional)
Glue

Directions:
1. Draw a picture of Moses going down the mountain, holding the Ten Commandments. Draw circles below the mountain to represent people. (Draw simple bodies if you like.)
2. Take a photo of each child looking happy or excited (or give the children markers and let them draw their happy faces on the circles). Cut out each child's face from the photo and let him glue it to a circle on the mural.
3. Ask the children why they think getting the Ten Commandments was a good thing.

0-382-30655-4

"THE SHADOW" STORY

Make a shadow box (see page 68) as you tell the story of "The Shadow." Following the story, let children make shadow boxes of their own.

"Ohhhhh," King Hezekiah groaned as he lay on his bed. He felt so sick.

"Get ready, Hezekiah," a visitor told the king. "You are going to die."

When the visitor left, Hezekiah felt so bad. He turned his face to the wall and cried and cried and cried.

"Dear God," the king prayed, "Please help me to get well."

Knock, knock, knock. The visitor had returned.

"King Hezekiah," the visitor said, "God has heard your prayers. He is going to make you well."

"How can I be sure?" asked the king.

"See the shadow on the stairway?" asked the visitor. "Do you want it to move up or down?"

"That shadow goes up every day," said the king. "Have the shadow move down if God will make me well."

"OK," said the visitor.

The shadow moved as Hezekiah watched. Slowly, slowly, slowly it moved down the stairway, down, down, down—ten whole steps.

Suddenly the king's heart felt very happy.

"God is going to make me well!" he said.

0-382-30655-4

SHADOW BOXES

Materials: A shoebox for each child
Copies of the pictures below
Glue

Directions:
1. Glue the pictures of Hezekiah in bed, Isaiah the visitor, and the stairs around the inside of the shoebox.
2. Review the story of Hezekiah. Emphasize that God made him well.

0-382-30655-4

MEMORY VERSE CRAFT

"... I will heal you ...." 2 Kings 20:5

Fig Leaf Craft

Directions:
1. Give each child a copy of the fig leaf picture below.
2. Have the children color the leaves green and the figs brown.
3. Glue the picture on construction paper.
4. Repeat the memory verse together.
5. Discuss how Jesus touched sick people and made them well.

cut ↑

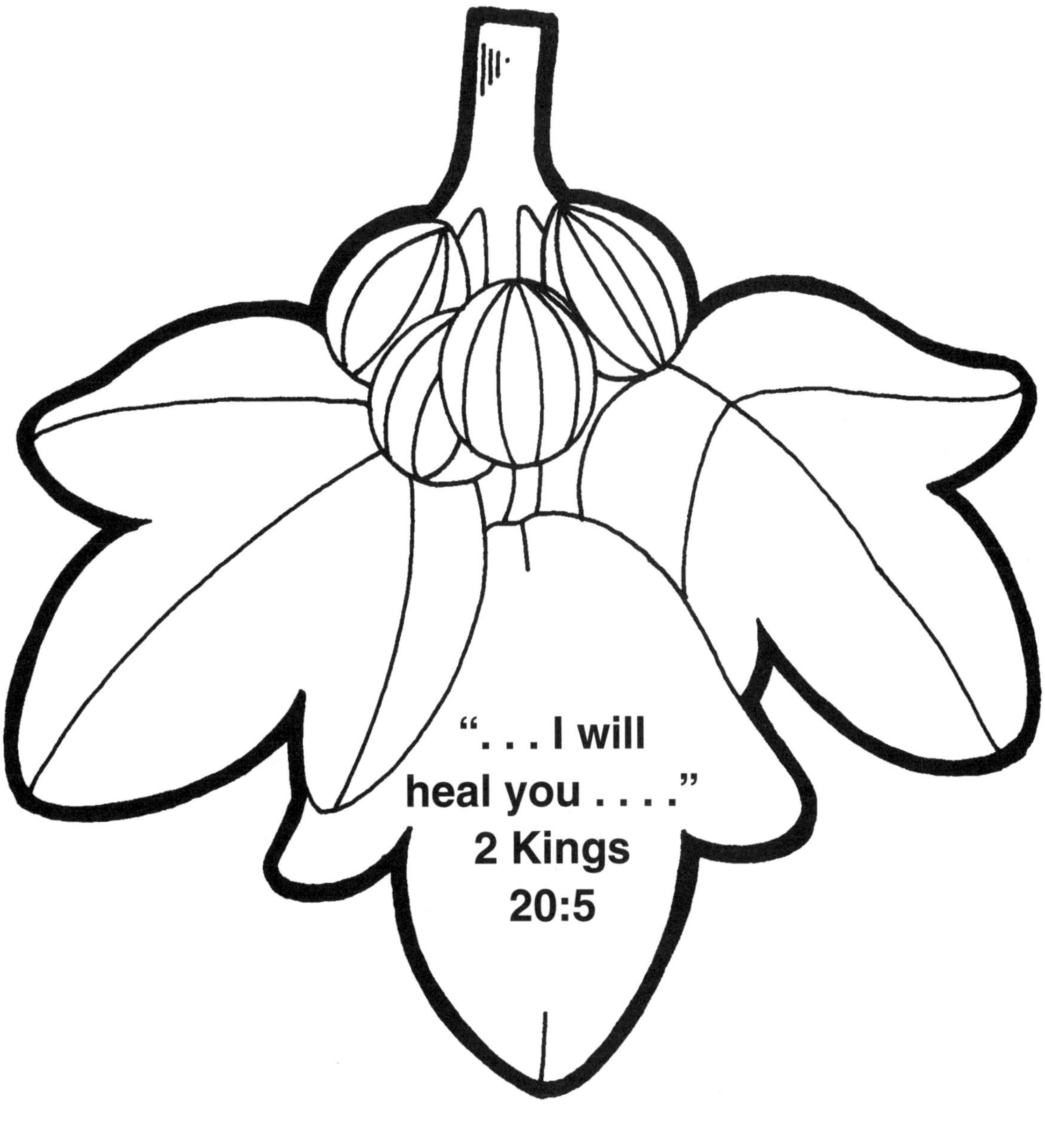

0-382-30655-4

SHADOW ART

Darken the room except for a strong flashlight or projector pointed toward a blank wall. Use your hands to make shadow animals. Explain that anything blocking the light casts a shadow. Discuss how God moved a shadow in an unusual way to let Hezekiah know he would get well. Let the children make shadow animals too.

A Bible Snack

Bring fresh figs, fig preserves, fig bars, or fig cookies to class. Explain that:

1. Figs are a type of soft fruit with many tiny seeds.
2. Figs grow on trees with broad green leaves.
3. People have used fig leaves for clothing and for shade.
4. In the story of Hezekiah, figs were used for medicine. Read 2 Kings 20:7.
5. People eat figs raw, in preserves, and in desserts.
6. Serve fig cookies and milk or fig preserves on toast.
7. Thank God for doctors, nurses, and medicines that keep us healthy.

KINDNESS MAZE

Tell the children that sick people really need to feel God's love. Children can help share God's love by being kind. Copy this page for all the children. Let them follow the fig maze to find kindnesses they can do for sick family members or friends.

0-382-30655-4

"WHEN I'M SICK, I PRAY" GAME

Seat children in a circle with the leader standing in the middle. Children hop up and exchange seats when the leader says something they do when they get sick.

1. When I'm sick, I take medicine.
2. When I'm sick, I sleep.
3. When I'm sick, I take my temperature.
4. When I'm sick, I listen to Bible stories.
5. When I'm sick, I stay in bed.
6. When I'm sick, I go to the doctor.
7. When I'm sick, I pray.

"Jesus Heals the Sick" Song

(Tune: Chorus of "Bringing in the Sheaves")

Jesus heals the sick.
Jesus heals the sick.
I am very thankful,
Jesus heals the sick. *(Repeat)*

Jesus loves me so.
Jesus loves me so.
I am very thankful,
Jesus loves me so. *(Repeat)*

Song Motions

Children join hands and walk in a circle to the right the first time through the song and to the left on the repeat.

PROJECT BAND-AID™

Bring a play doctor kit and a box of Band-Aids™ to class. Discuss how God often uses doctors and nurses and medicine to help us get well.

Give a Band-Aid™ to each child to unwrap and play with. Talk about cuts and bruises that slowly heal and disappear under a Band-Aid™. Tell the class that God made our bodies special to help most of our cuts and bruises heal naturally.

Review Questions

1. What was wrong with King Hezekiah? *(He had a sore that made him sick.)*
2. Why did the king cry and pray? *(No one could make him well.)*
3. What did the visitor tell him? *(God would make him well.)*
4. How did Hezekiah know God would answer his prayers? *(God moved a shadow backwards.)*
5. Have you ever been sick?
6. Did you ask God to make you well?

Bedtime Reminder

Before we sleep, *(Hands at side of head like a pillow.)*
We say our prayers *(Hands folded in prayer.)*
For all sick children *(Hand on forehead.)*
Everywhere. *(Hands spread far apart.)*
God bless . . . . *(Let the children name sick people for whom they can pray.)*

DOORKNOB HANGER

Materials: Poster paper
Watercolor paints or crayons
Paintbrushes
Copy of doorknob hanger on page 75 for each child
Crayons

Directions:
1. Using the pattern on page 75, trace and cut out a doorknob hanger from poster board for each child.
2. Color and put designs on the doorknob hanger with crayons.
3. Color and cut out the pattern below.
4. Glue the pattern to the doorknob hanger.
5. Say the memory verse, "I will heal you," together.

DOORKNOB HANGER PATTERN

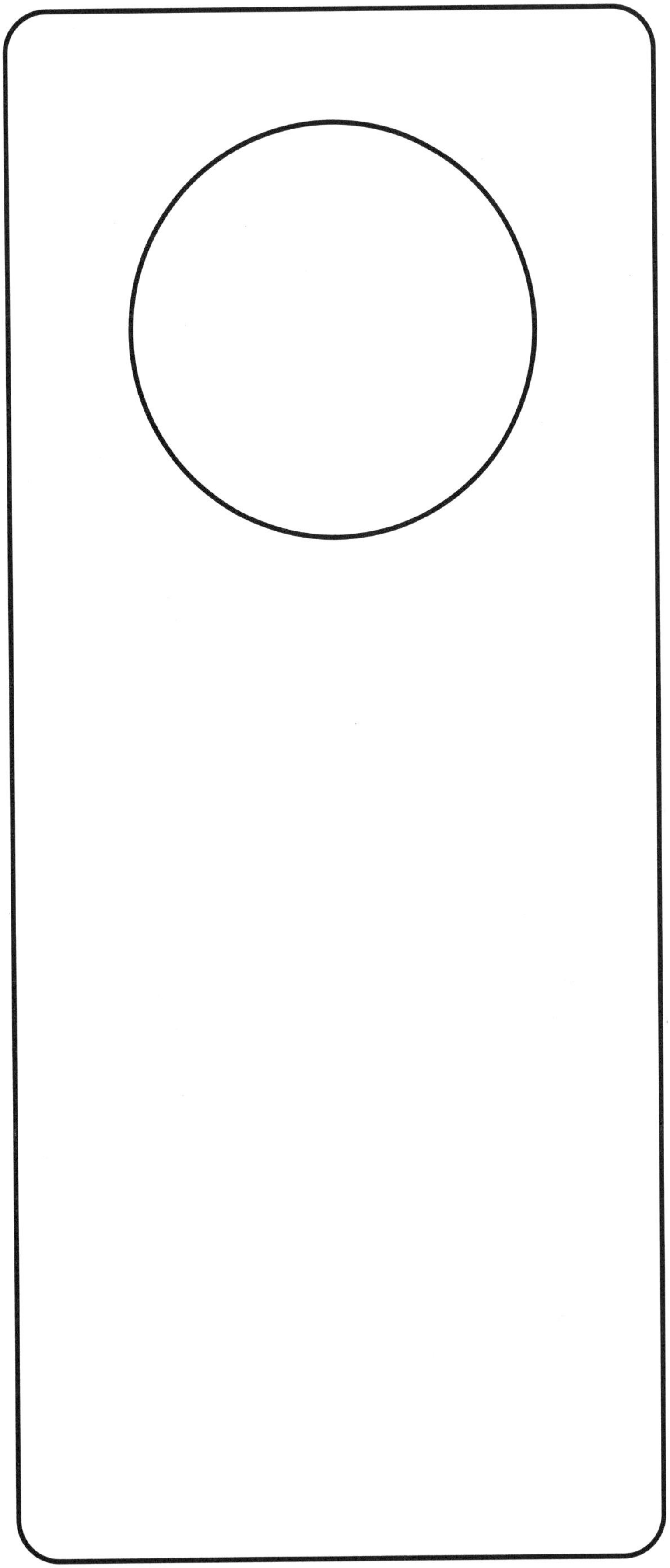

0-382-30655-4

SHADOW PICTURE OF JESUS

Copy and cut out the pattern of Jesus below for each child. Tape the figure to a piece of black paper. Let each child color all over the paper with a white crayon or chalk. Lift off the figure and see the shadow print that is left on the paper. Remind children that Jesus healed many sick people—those who could not see, hear, talk or walk; mommies, daddies, boys, and girls. We should say thank You to Him for making sick people well.

0-382-30655-4

THE STORY OF HANNAH

Moving Pictures

Copy and cut out the figures of Happy Hannah, Sad Hannah, Peninnah, Hannah's husband, and Eli on pages 78-79. Tape the figures to the sides of paper cups turned upside down. Move the picture cups around on a table as you tell "The Story of Hannah." Place Baby Samuel (backed with tape) in Happy Hannah's arms at the end of the story.

The Story of Hannah

"Boo, hoo, hoo. Boo, hoo, hoo." Hannah is very sad. She won't eat. She can't sleep. She cries all the time.

"Boo, hoo, hoo. Boo, hoo, hoo." Peninnah teases Hannah for crying.

"Don't tease me anymore!" says Hannah. Then she cries even more.

"What's wrong, Hannah?" asks her husband. "Why are you crying all the time?"

"I'm so sad," says Hannah. "I have no children."

"I'm sorry," says her husband. He gives Hannah a hug.

After supper Hannah walks to God's house. She kneels to pray. "Please, dear God," she asks, "Please, give me a little son. Then one day when he is bigger, I will give him back to You."

Mr. Eli, God's helper, watches Hannah. He wonders why she cries and cries and cries.

"I am praying about a big problem," Hannah tells him.

"Well, wipe your tears and cheer up," says Mr. Eli. "God will help you solve your problem."

Suddenly Hannah feels much better. "Yes, that's right," she says. She wipes her tears. She hurries home.

Before long, God answers Hannah's prayer. He gives Hannah a baby boy. She names him Samuel. Then Hannah laughs and laughs and laughs. At last she is a happy, happy mother.

Isn't God great? He listens when we pray!

0-382-30655-4

MOVING PICTURE PATTERNS

Hannah

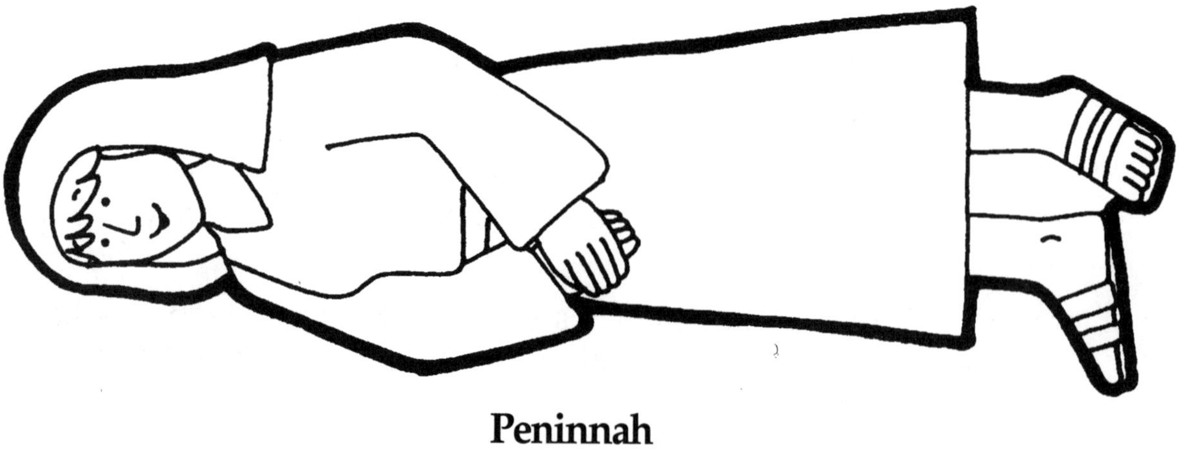

Peninnah

MOVING PICTURE PATTERNS

Hannah's Husband

Eli

Baby Samuel

0-382-30655-4

PRAYER BEAR MOBILES

Materials: Six Prayer Bears (two of each kind from below and page 81) per child
- Stapler
- String
- Coat hanger
- Crayons or markers

Directions:
1. Copy, cut out, and color the bears.
2. Fold two matching bears on the dotted lines.
3. Put the two bears back to back and staple them in the center of the fold.
4. Fan out the sides like four butterfly wings.
5. Attach a string to the top with tape.
6. Hang the Prayer Bear on a coat hanger.
7. Follow the same directions with the other two bears.
8. Display the mobile and talk about how we can pray anywhere, any time, about anything.
9. Make a mobile for each child or use it as a group project.

PRAYER BEAR PATTERNS

0-382-30655-4

MEMORY VERSE REMINDER

Copy two praying Hannah pictures for each child. Have the children color and cut them out. Glue them on either side of an upside down paper cup. Recite the memory verse printed on Hannah's skirt. Tell the children to display their prayer reminders at home.

0-382-30655-4

PICTURE PRAYER SCROLL

Materials: A 12" strip of adding machine tape for each child
Two unsharpened pencils for each child
Tape
A copy of the picture strip below for each child

Directions:
1. Give each child a 12" strip of adding machine paper.
2. Help the child cut apart the picture strip of people for whom they can pray.
3. Glue the pictures on the 12" strip.
4. Tape a pencil to each end of the paper strip.
5. Roll the paper on the pencils to make a scroll.
6. Discuss how we can pray for others.

0-382-30655-4

PRAYER CARDS

Materials: Pastel colored construction paper
Scissors
Crayons
Envelopes and stamps
Scrap pieces of felt
Buttons
Lace (optional)

Directions:

1. Trace each child's hand on a piece of folded paper or use the praying hands pattern below. Be sure to place the correct side of the hand on the fold line of the paper.
2. Cut out the praying hands, being careful not to cut on the fold line.
3. Ask each child to name someone for whom they will pray.
4. Inside the praying hands card, write, "Dear ________________, I am praying for you today."
5. Help the child sign his name on the card.
6. Glue lace trim, felt for a cuff, or a button as shown on the front of the card.
7. Put each prayer card in an envelope.
8. Mail it to the person the child selected, or send it home for parents to mail.

"I CAN PRAY" SONG

Introduce the song by telling the children they can pray anywhere—at a party, at the zoo, on a bicycle, in a tree house. Let them name some places they pray. Sing the song through several times until the children are familiar with it. Then pass out rhythm instruments or make the "Shaker Plates" described below for children to play as they sing.

I Can Pray

(Tune: "Jingle Bells")

I can pray, I can pray
Every night and day.

I can pray, I can pray
At work or at play.

I can pray, I can pray
Everything's okay.

I can pray, I can pray
God hears the words I say.

Shaker Plates

Materials: Two paper plates for each child
Dry beans
Tape
Crepe paper streamers

Directions:
1. Tape two plates together with several dry beans between them.
2. Add crepe paper streamers on the edges.
3. Beat the plates with a hand like a tambourine or shake them to keep rhythm with the song.

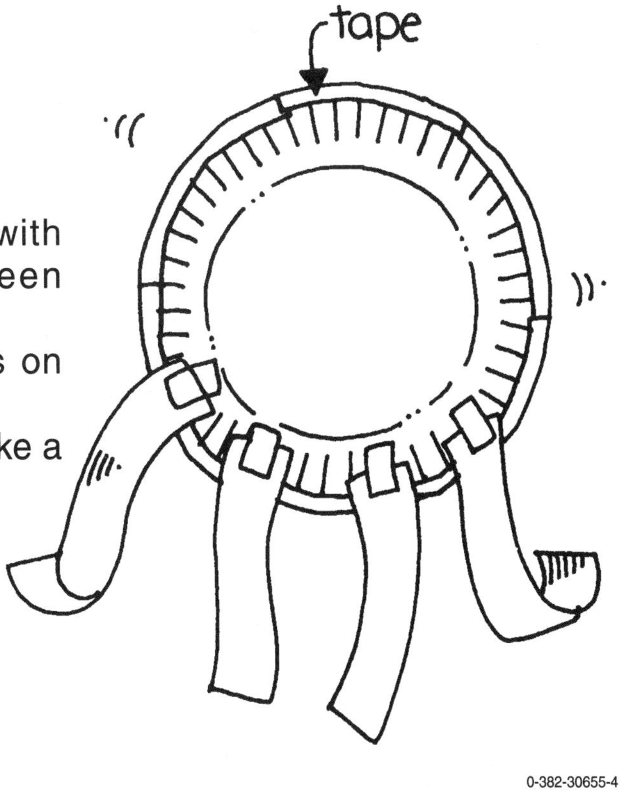

0-382-30655-4

HAPPY HANNAH ACTION SONG

(Tune: "Eency Weency Spider")

Directions:
1. On the first line of the action song, children walk in place.
2. On line two, children put their hands together to pray.
3. On line three, they swoosh their fears away.
4. On line four, children run in place.

Song

Hannah went to God's house one day.
Up came her hands when Hannah prayed.
Down came the tears and washed her fears away.
And happy, happy Hannah ran home okay.

Review Questions

1. Why was Hannah crying? *(She had no little children.)*
2. Where did Hannah go? *(To God's House)*
3. What did Hannah do at God's house? *(She prayed.)*
4. Did God answer Hannah's prayers? *(Yes, he did!)*
5. What did God give Hannah? *(A baby boy)*
6. Will God listen when we pray? *(Yes, He always hears our prayers.)*

Finger Play and Prayer

Use the following finger play as an introduction to group prayer. Lead children in thank-You prayers, or asking prayers or telling prayers. Encourage all children to participate.

Put your hands together *(Fold hands in prayer.)*
To start a special prayer.
Then close your eyes and whisper, *(Close eyes.)*
And Jesus will be there.
God bless . . . .

"IN MY FATHER'S HOUSE" STORY

Dramatize the Bible Story

Read the Bible story several times to practice telling it dramatically. Give the children simple Biblical costumes such as scarves and headbands to wear. Tell the Bible story, playing the part of Mary. Have the children mimic your actions at the asterisks. You may prefer to enlarge the pictures and use them to illustrate the story.

In My Father's House

*Tromp, tromp, tromp. *(Walk in place.)* Mary and Joseph were walking home. The party was over. The trip was long. All the people were tired.

"I'll get Jesus," Mary told Joseph. "We can stop by the road and eat our dinner."

"Fine," said Joseph. "I haven't seen Him all day long."

*"Have you seen Jesus?" *(Cup hands around mouth.)* Mary called to the other children.

"No," they said. "We have not seen Him all day long."

*"Oh, no! *(Shake head.)* Jesus is missing!" *(Hands on face.)* Mary told Joseph.

While their friends walked home, Mary and Joseph walked back to the busy city.

*For three days Mary and Joseph looked for Jesus *(Turn left and right, hands over eyes.)* in the shops, in the streets. Finally, they looked in God's house. There, among the teachers, sat one happy, little boy. And who do you think He was?

*"Jesus!" his mom and dad called. "We have looked everywhere for you!" *(Pat legs with hands.)*

"Well, didn't you know I had to be in My Father's house?" Jesus said.

*Mary hugged Jesus tightly. *(Hug self.)* She was happy that Jesus was safe in God's house.

0-382-30655-4

BIBLE STORY PICTURES

FOOTSTEP MAZE

Materials: Construction paper
Scissors
Tape
Temple picture (below)
Footprint pattern (below)

Directions:
1. Cut out ten (or more) footprints.
2. Tape the footprints in a path on the classroom floor, leading to God's House (an enlarged picture of the temple taped to the wall).
3. Let the children follow the path to find Jesus, learning at the temple.

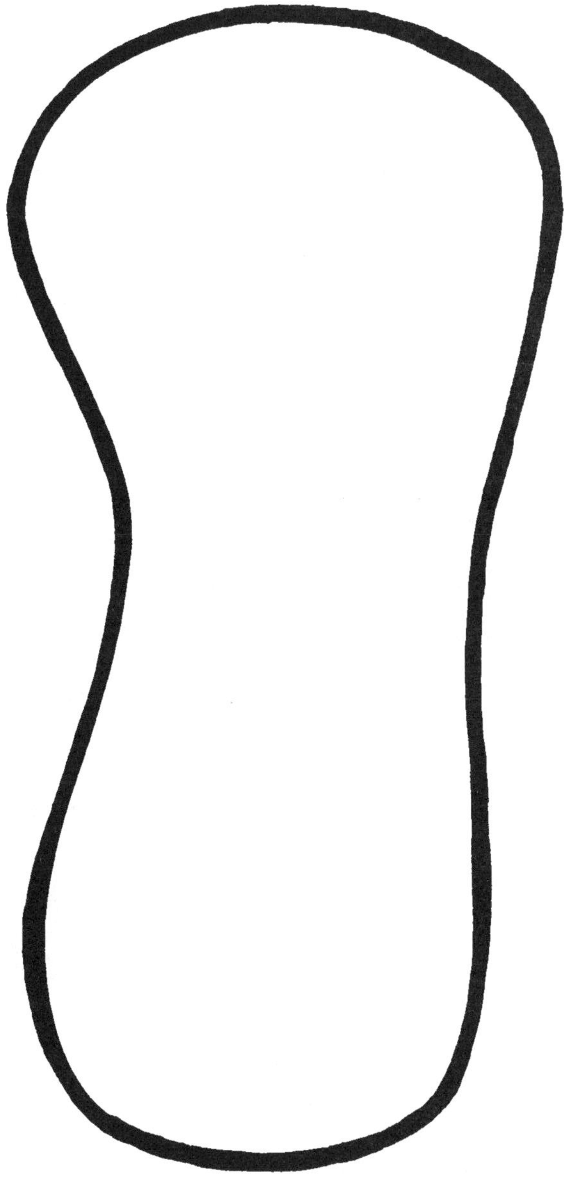

LESSON QUESTIONS ABOUT GOD'S HOUSE

1. Where were Mary and Joseph going?	*(Home)*
2. Who was missing?	*(Jesus)*
3. Where did Mary and Joseph find Him?	*(In God's house)*
4. What was Jesus doing?	*(Learning about God)*
5. What do you do in God's house?	*(Talk with God and learn about Him)*

Finger Play

Thank You, God,	*(Lace fingers inward.)*
For making the church	*(Lift and match pointers, pinkies, and thumbs.)*
A special place	*(Keeping thumbs together, pointed downward, unlace other fingers and curve them into a heart.)*
I love so much!	

In God's House with Motions

(Tune: "Three Blind Mice")

In God's house,	*(clap, clap, clap)*
In God's house,	*(clap, clap, clap)*
Jesus went.	*(tromp, tromp, tromp)*
Jesus went.	*(tromp, tromp, tromp)*
He wanted to learn all the things he could.	*(circle right)*
So He could help the neighborhood.	*(circle left)*
Don't you think that was good?	*(shake hands with neighbor)*
In God's house.	*(tromp, tromp, tromp)*

0-382-30655-4

SOMEONE'S MISSING

Play hide-and-seek. Laminate a picture of Jesus. Choose a child to be "it." Let "it" hide a picture of Jesus while the other children turn their backs. Then the children pretend to be Mary and Joseph looking for Him. Tell the children that Jesus' favorite place was in God's house.

0-382-30655-4

CHURCH: A PLACE TO WORK FOR GOD
SPONGE-PAINTED PRAYER AND PROMISE

Materials: Construction paper
Small decorative shapes cut from sponges
A copy of the prayer (page 93) and promise (below) for each child

Directions:
1. Glue the prayer on a piece of construction paper.
2. Read the prayer to the children.
3. Blot the sponge, filled with paint, around the edges of the prayer.
4. Follow the same instructions for the promise.

A Prayer

God bless my teachers
Every day
In all they do
At work or play.

Help them to teach me
Of Your love,
And of Your Son
Who lives above.

PUPPET TALK

Prepare Newsy the Puppet before class.

Materials: Newspaper
Tape
Markers
Scissors

Directions:
1. Roll a sheet of newspaper into a tight cylinder. Tape it together.
2. Make three cuts, one-fourth of the way down the cylinder from the top.
3. Partially uncurl the inside of the cylinder by pulling the cut strips upward. The cut strips make the puppet's bushy hair.
4. Draw a face on the puppet.
5. Use the dialogue below to teach the children that the church is a place of prayer.

Newsy: "Hi, boys and girls! My name is Newsy the Puppet. What are your names?"

Newsy: "On Sundays I go to church. I meet new friends. I learn about God. I talk to Him. What do you do at church?"

Newsy: "Jesus wants the church to be a place to talk to God. Why don't we get your teacher to talk to God right now?" *(Teacher prays, thanking God for the church and the children.)*

Newsy: "Well, gotta go! Good-bye, boys and girls."

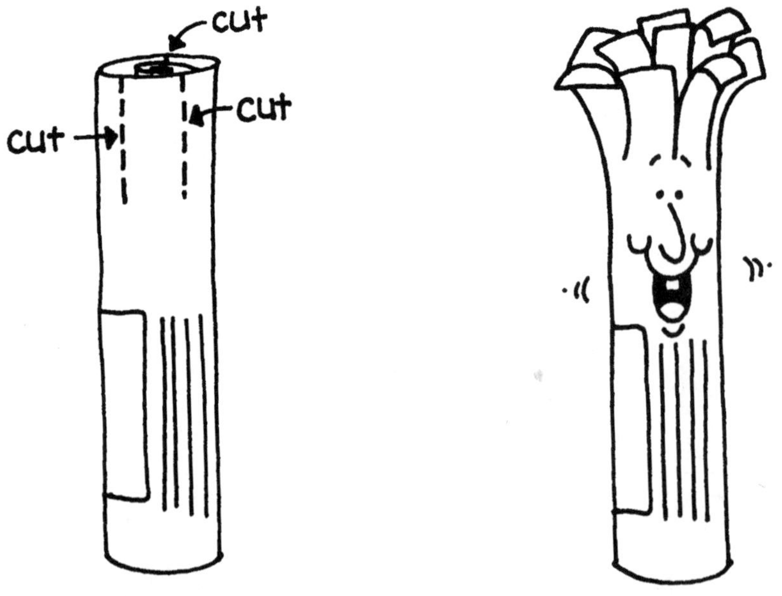

MEMORY VERSE BUILDING BLOCKS

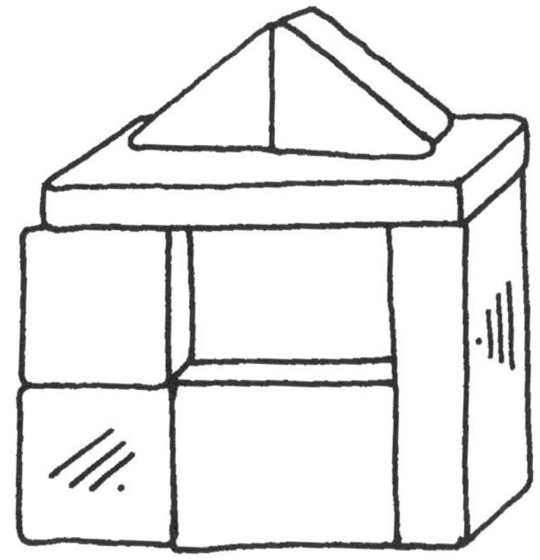

Materials: Wooden building blocks

Directions:
1. Say the memory verse together.
2. Stack wooden blocks to build a church.
3. Discuss why people build churches.

Memory Verse

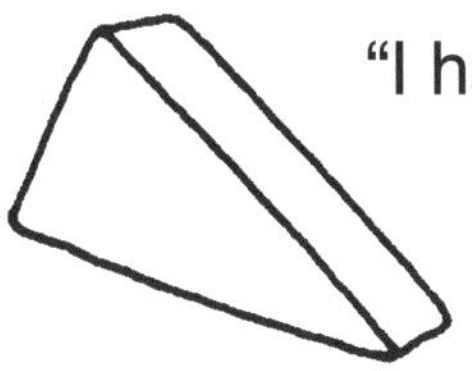

"I had to be in my Father's House." Luke 2:49b

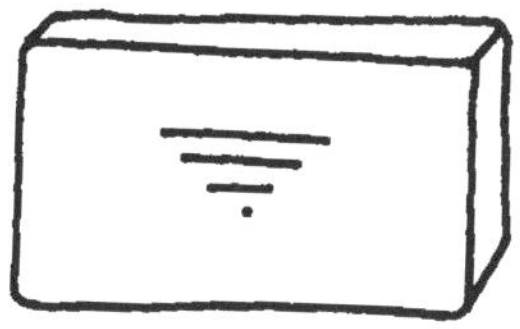

Church Workers

Discuss what people do in God's house like sing; pray; and learn about God, Jesus, the Holy Spirit, the Bible.

Discuss church workers—choir members, ushers, teachers, preachers, nursery workers.

Let the children draw pictures of workers they might be in the church when they grow up. Remind them that they work for God when they help their parents, pastor, and teachers.

Jesus Loves the Church

(Tune: "Row, Row, Row Your Boat")

Jesus loves the church,
Loves the church so much.
He made many people,
Telling of His love.

CONCENTRATION GAME

Directions:
1. Duplicate and cut out two each of the cards below.
2. Place the cards face down and in rows on the table.
3. Let the children take turns trying to find matches.
4. When someone finds a match, the two cards become his.
5. Play until all the cards are matched.

Minister

Organist

Nursery Worker

Teacher

Usher

Choir Member